Robert W. Richardson's

RIO GRANDE

— Chasing the Narrow Gauge —

VOLUME II

Dedication

To the Railroaders of the Narrow Gauge
who tolerated and often encouraged railfans in the observation and exploration of their lines.

ACKNOWLEDGEMENTS

Upon retiring in 1991 I gave my 60-year collection of negatives and slides to the Western History Department of the Denver Public Library. Augie Mastrogiuseppe, curator of photographs, had plans to use the collection as one means to promote the extensive collection of the Department. His sudden demise ended that program.

This volume is not intended as a history of these lines, but instead provides a view of them the way they were in their final decades of operation. Friends have contributed photographs from their experiences, and I wish to thank Mallory Hope Ferrell, Arthur W. Wallace, the family of the late Clayton Tanner, Dr. Richard Severance, Lee Monroe and Don Heimburger.

Library of Congress Control Number: 2004112829
ISBN: 0-911581-57-X
First Edition
Printed in Hong Kong

HEIMBURGER HOUSE PUBLISHING COMPANY
7236 West Madison Street
Forest Park, Illinois 60130

Editing: Donald J. Heimburger; Book design: Rachel L. Boger
Cover: Locomotive #223 at Baldwin, Colorado. *Gil Bennett painting*; Endsheet photography: Robert W. Richardson, Western History Department, Denver Public Library collection; unless otherwise noted, all photographs are by Robert W. Richardson, courtesy of the Western History Department, Denver Public Library.

CONTENTS

Durango, Silverton, Farmington & the Third Division

Engine #481 slumbers in the darkened Durango roundhouse between runs in the summer of 2004. *Don Heimburger*

A LONG, DRAWN-OUT VANISHING ACT

When I located at Alamosa in 1948, the operations of the Narrow Gauge seemed timeless, having changed little over the years. Perhaps management had been intimidated by all the trouble their abandonment of the Chili Line in 1941 had brought upon them. And they'd hardly relaxed when the following year the military wanted to requisition some items for use in Alaska, which seemed to give them an opportunity to shut down, and again a public uproar forced them to continue operations.

This volume is the story of what I found in 1948, with a big spurt of business in 1951-52, gradually beginning the narrow gauge's final and long drawn-out vanishing act, except for two successful tourist operations.

The Narrow Gauge Circle was still complete, rails on the three major operations were kept polished, and many miles were no more rusty or weedier than in past years. Two or three times each week freights ambled over the Alamosa-Durango line. And much of the year, daily or even double daily turns worked the Monarch Branch.

A mixed train to Silverton had enough business to run a couple of times a week, despite spring flooding and winter slides. Over at Montrose, a narrow gauge engine was yard switcher for both gauges, and Mudhens made connections with the Rio Grande Southern, while one of the last 2-8-0 types went to Ouray as needed, at least every month at the lowest ebb of the mine output.

Rustiest of all the lines was that beyond Sapinero, where once a month a freight ventured to Montrose, displaying with its doubling or even tripling Cerro Hill, the way things were in busier times. And the most senior crews enjoyed the two-day roundtrip on the Valley Line, also occuring but once a month.

The other important all-narrow gauge terminal in 1948 was Gunnison. Its once busy roundhouse now sheltered just three or four Consolidations. Mudhens once so active there were long gone. What kept Gunnison alive was the coal traffic from Crested Butte to Salida, where it was transferred to standard gauge cars and onto the steel works at Pueblo.

Changes in steel making and the growing availability of the right kind of coal from new mines at the steel company's subsidiary west of Trinidad pointed in 1948 to a questionable future for the Crested Butte mine.

By 1952 the Big Mine at Crested Butte was finished. Aside from seasonal stock trains, there was only some lumber and the household coal from Baldwin. And gas lines were encroaching on that market.

Because of a light bridge, the last two Class C-16s were kept at Gunnison for the Baldwin Branch, a relic of the vanished South Park. The pair of C-21 outside-frame 2-8-0s were ample to handle the monthly freight to Montrose. Extensive earth slides on the western side of Cerro Summit gave the railroad the only solution, to abandon the track through the Black Canyon west of Sapinero. In the summer of 1949 work trains removed the rails to within a few miles of Montrose. The result was that when the two ex-Crystal River engines needed repairs, they were sent dead to Salida for scrapping.

Toward the last, in the early 1950s, with one C-16 gone to the Chicago Railroad Fair in 1948-49 (#268 in the Bumblebee paint scheme), only well-worn #278 remained at Gunnison. Once in a while a K-36 for a coal train would share the otherwise empty building.

Even the little #278 saw little use after 1950. With abandonment of the Cerro Summit line and the Valley Line in 1951, Baldwin coal could no longer reach its two good markets of Alamosa and Montrose. What business remained was handled by an occasional trucker.

Abandonment of all the Gunnison lines west of Poncha Junction came late in 1954, the public hearing featuring virtually no opposition—no one could promise the tonnage that was needed for the lines to stay alive. So during the summer of 1955, the Western State College football team was employed by the rail dismantlers with at least one happy result for Gunnison: that fall the team romped all over the opposition after three months of loading heavy rails.

So it was that Durango became the all-narrow gauge center, surviving after the various final runs of the postwar years.

In 1951 Durango saw a great reduction in its importance and a resulting drop in activity. On January 31 the *San Juan* had made its final run. Much of the summer there were no RGS trains, as the Highway Department placed a span in the Franklin Junction trestle just outside town. There were very few excursion runs that year on the RGS using the Goose, just several late in the summer.

In the summer, Hollywood made the film *Denver & Rio Grande* using the last two Consolidations on hand to fake a head-on collision in the Animas Canyon. Thereafter, switching was done by one of the Class K-28 #470 series engines or Mudhen #453.

Mudhen Class K-27 engines saw a further decline in their numbers as #452 was set aside, eventually to go to scrap, its tender used in 1952 by the rail dismantlers of the RGS as a water car. The engine was used on the November 1951 last run from Rico to Durango, then set aside.

Mudhen #453 continued that year to be the Durango switcher with #463 used on the Silverton runs.

An unusual visitor to Durango briefly that summer was C-16 #268 which had been brought from Gunnison for use in the movie and then quickly returned. It had quite a trip, via standard gauge flat car from Salida to Alamosa before returning to narrow gauge rails at that point.

Durangoans generally continued to ignore the Silverton train, which at the height of the summer handled sellout crowds and turned quite a few away. For several years management held two coaches at Alamosa instead of forwarding them to Durango. It was alleged they were kept at Alamosa so that in the event of an accident they could haul doctors to the scene. That accident never occurred.

Eastbound freights included cars destined to be scrapped, reducing the freight rolling stock to just about 1,000 cars, despite the growing pipe traffic needs. The final RGS freights brought in many empties from the isolated Ouray Branch, and these, too, were forwarded to Alamosa.

In 1948 we didn't know that the railroad had made plans to rid itself of all branches, and that it tried to become a bridge carrier across the two states. The 2,578 freight cars in a few years would shrink to less than half that. The 42 locomotives would become 20, with all Consolidations gone. And 32 narrow gauge passenger cars declined to a mere 10. By 1956, only the Alamosa-Durango-Farmington-Silverton lines remained.

On the Fourth of July weekend in 1941, the Silverton train had but two passengers, and they were only one-way tickets that cost 2 cents per mile.

Now, 60 some years later, the trains are all passenger, often running in two or three sections, each with 350 or so aboard, and fares run in the $60 range for roundtrips. Old passenger cars set aside as bodies, or for housing work crews, have been rebuilt like new at costs exceeding $100,000 per car, so a 10-car train represents a $1 million investment. Sixty years ago the track was kept up just well enough to handle the infrequent trains, and is now equal to the best of tracks, the result of years of upgrading.

When I bought caboose #0500 in 1949, when it was scheduled to be burned for its scrap metal, no one would have expected that weary-looking car to be seen in 2004 as a special car for charter on the Silverton, looking no doubt even better than it did when it was new 122 years ago.

The grades of the Gunnison lines have vanished into scenic byways in places like Marshall Pass, and the trip through the Black Canyon has become a scenic boat trip arranged by the National Park Service for its Curecanti Recreational Area patrons.

The result is that tourist travel through Colorado has become something far beyond the dreams of Major Shadrach K. Hooper who advertised the wonders of the state in hundreds of thousands of descriptive booklets, intending to entice travelers to travel by the D&RG.

We'll relive some of my memories of these narrow gauge lines in this volume, and see scenes from long-ago railroading in the Rockies. I hope you'll enjoy it.

Bob Richardson at Sargent, Colorado in September of 2003 with the Sargent water tank and a few other railroad structures still in tact in the background. *Gordon Chappell*

In this general view of the Durango yard, Engine #315 switches the *San Juan* passenger train in 1949. In the left background is Perins Peak, to which point a branch line was built off the Rio Grande Southern in 1901 to reach a coal mine, which was operated until 1926.

One

DURANGO YARD, ONE OF THE MOST EXPLORED

Probably the most explored railroad yard in Colorado is the yard at Durango. As tourists began to come in numbers to ride the Silverton train, many of them would walk around the yard, peer into the roundhouse and curiously examine the assortment of idle engines and cars cluttering up the place.

One of the frustrations of the Perlman administration in the early 1950s was confronting the growing number of visitors in railroad yards. The administration was incensed that visitors would engage the employees in conversation, certainly reducing the amount of time spent in work. In the summer of 1952 came an edict from Denver to the foreman and trainmaster to keep visitors out of the yard and roundhouse, and if they refused to leave, to remove them forcibly.

After a few days of arguments, indignant protestations and attempts to escort visitors out, the foreman gave up, as his help was spending too much time in this pursuit. As most of the Silverton's passengers were unfamiliar with railroads, often this being the first train they had ever ridden, they looked on the entire railroad as a tour-ist attraction and felt, consequently, that they should be able to stroll around as they pleased. As for the employees, they sort of enjoyed having an audience watch them working the turntable and otherwise engaged in their hostling duties.

For the railfan, the yard had a considerable fascination. When the line opened in 1881 there was the customary wye, eventually lost and replaced by a loop on which the daily *San Juan* and Silverton trains were turned. North of the depot were storage tracks in what was originally the alley area behind the main street. In later decades the business district expanded beyond these tracks, and the alley became dignified with the name of Narrow Gauge Avenue—and parking meters.

A yard crew was on duty employing a variety of the smaller engines—various classes of 2-8-0 types. Some well-known engines of later times spent much of their latter life as Durango switchers, including Nos. 268, 315, 319, 345 and 346. As these small engines vanished from the scene, the K-28 470 series then did the work. The assigned switch engine could always be identified with the toolbox placed on top of the cab. The smaller engines exchanged their pilots for footboards.

This is a general view from the coal dock at Durango. The *San Juan* and Silverton Mixed are at the depot. Yard engine #315 is at lower right, and the big plow pilot at center is waiting for winter when it will be placed on a Mudhen.

There was a coaling dock at Durango like those at Gunnison and Chama and a huge water tank with spouts on both sides. In revamping the yard for the Durango & Silverton Narrow Gauge Railroad, these were removed, and significantly, the pumphouse for the tank was removed too. This was a mistake realized only when the roundhouse was destroyed in a fire, and firemen could not find a hydrant close by.

On trackage south of the water tank, outgoing freights were made up and incoming ones set out. Like all the narrow gauge yards, there wasn't any surplus trackage, so extra switching was required. Cabooses were set out on one of the tracks opposite the depot. Out-of-service items

were shoved into a steep track along the hillside, a remnant of a long spur that at one time reached a coal mine.

The RGS track ended at a point near the west bank of the river, the bridge and smelter trackage being D&RGW. Departing RGS trains had to back down the yard to the switch from which they could drop down to the bridge and on west. The outside tracks of the turntable would usually have a spare Goose sitting there. At the end of one of these tracks might be the huge snowplow ready to be bolted to a Mudhen. A couple of the roundhouse tracks served as a shop area with various machine tools nearby. An odd sort of lean-to on the depot side included a small office

Engine #315 was the yard engine at Durango in 1949, seen here switching the *San Juan*. Shortly after a crack was found in a cylinder, the engine was set aside in Durango for display, with a balloon stack, something it never had. Severely vandalized, it is now being rebuilt by the Durango Railroad Historical Society.

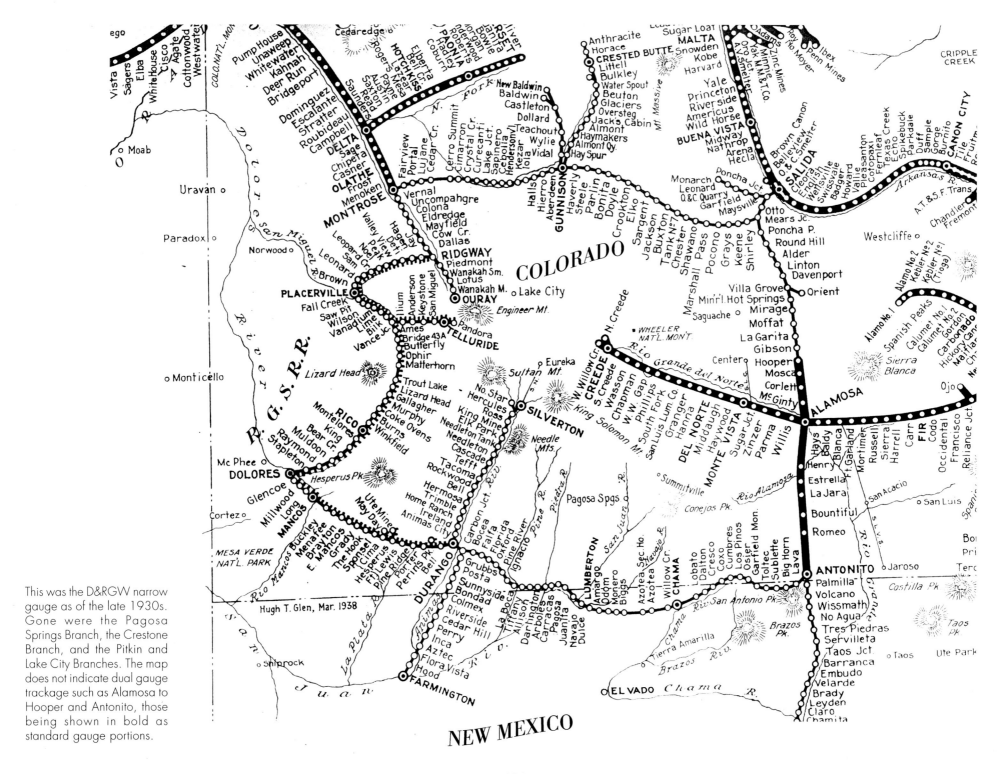

This was the D&RGW narrow gauge as of the late 1930s. Gone were the Pagosa Springs Branch, the Crestone Branch, and the Pitkin and Lake City Branches. The map does not indicate dual gauge trackage such as Alamosa to Hooper and Antonito, those being shown in bold as standard gauge portions.

Hugh T. Glen, Mar. 1938

COLORADO

NEW MEXICO

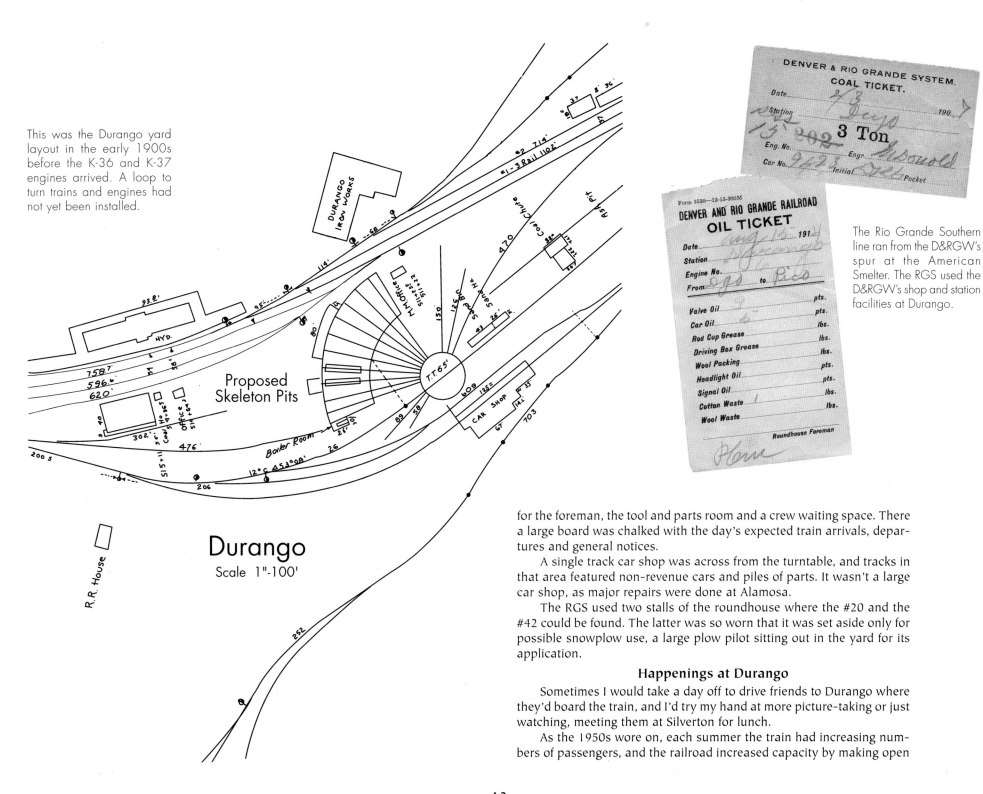

This was the Durango yard layout in the early 1900s before the K-36 and K-37 engines arrived. A loop to turn trains and engines had not yet been installed.

Proposed Skeleton Pits

DURANGO IRON WORKS

R.R. House

Durango
Scale 1"-100'

DENVER & RIO GRANDE SYSTEM.
COAL TICKET.
Date_____ 190_
Station_____
3 Ton
Eng. No._____ Engr._____
Car No._____ Initial_____ Pocket_____

Form 3530—12-13-300M
DENVER AND RIO GRANDE RAILROAD
OIL TICKET
Date_____ 191_
Station_____
Engine No._____
From_____ to_____

Valve Oil	pts.
Car Oil	pts.
Rod Cup Grease	lbs.
Driving Box Grease	lbs.
Wool Packing	pts.
Headlight Oil	pts.
Signal Oil	lbs.
Cotton Waste	lbs.
Wool Waste	lbs.

Roundhouse Foreman

The Rio Grande Southern line ran from the D&RGW's spur at the American Smelter. The RGS used the D&RGW's shop and station facilities at Durango.

for the foreman, the tool and parts room and a crew waiting space. There a large board was chalked with the day's expected train arrivals, departures and general notices.

A single track car shop was across from the turntable, and tracks in that area featured non-revenue cars and piles of parts. It wasn't a large car shop, as major repairs were done at Alamosa.

The RGS used two stalls of the roundhouse where the #20 and the #42 could be found. The latter was so worn that it was set aside only for possible snowplow use, a large plow pilot sitting out in the yard for its application.

Happenings at Durango

Sometimes I would take a day off to drive friends to Durango where they'd board the train, and I'd try my hand at more picture-taking or just watching, meeting them at Silverton for lunch.

As the 1950s wore on, each summer the train had increasing numbers of passengers, and the railroad increased capacity by making open

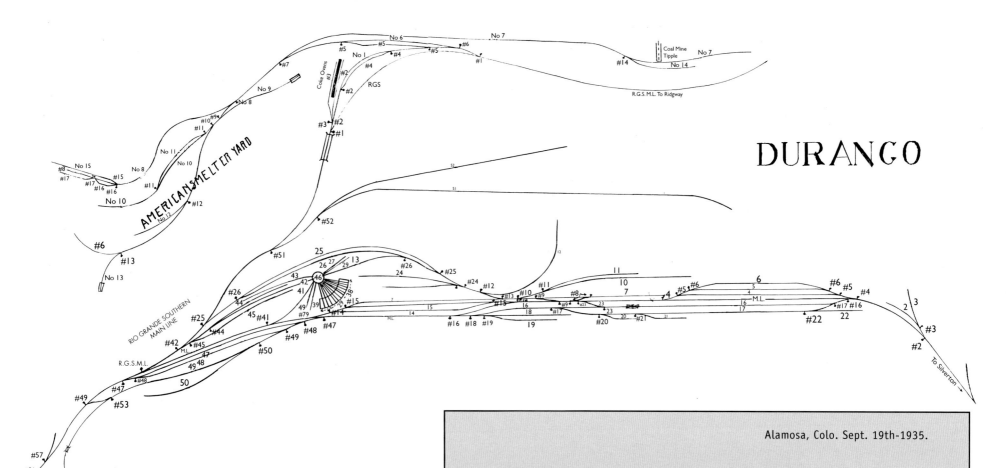

DURANGO

The numbers indicate identifying numbers for the Engineering Department to refer to when any work or changes were to be made; each track had a number same as its switch.

This page is from the schedule of livestock shipments for one of the last stock seasons on the Narrow Gauge. The heading features the following: Date of intended shipment, the number assigned to the loading, the first column gives the number assigned for a loading on the D&RGW, the next column the number assigned for a loading on the RGS.

"SD" indicates single deck cars are required; "DD" indicates double deck cars are required (for sheep); the single deck cars were for cattle.

The destination is given so that all concerned can plan ahead for the transfer to standard gauge cars and the proper feeding and watering of the animals. Shippers' names are given so that if the animals are late in being ready for loading, the shipper can be located; also in the event any other problem might arise.

On shipments from the RGS, a number was assigned for both railroads. The dispatchers plan these dates, etc. months ahead of the six week or so fall "stock rush." The D&RGW had 350 stock cars, and it took careful planning to have the correct type of cars at the loading points. The railroad also had to plan ahead and reserve standard gauge cars at the transfer points. For example: the October 1 loading at Silverton of 38 doubledeck cars of sheep would likely have moved east from Durango doubleheaded, and upon arrival at Chama, would be moved in one train up Cumbres with four engines, one engine handling the train on into Alamosa.

On that same date, the RGS would load 10 cattle at Dolores, the doubleheader then picking up four sheep DDs at Glencoe from Mr. Schlegel and four other DD loads from Mr. Honaker. The train then went on to make a brief stop at Mancos for three DD loads there. A third locomotive likely was waiting at Mancos to help the train at least to Cima, from which point the two Helpers would run light into Durango.

At Durango the D&RGW would likely have ready two engines to handle the 21 cars into Chama, where a third engine would be added to make a three-engine trip up Cumbres. Two of the engines would likely then drop back to Chama, the other engine taking the train on into Alamosa. In preparation for stock season, foremen would try to have all locomotives possible ready for use. Major repairs were always done before the beginning of the rush. The rotary snowplows at Alamosa and Chama were checked and made ready in August, just in case an early storm should cause trouble over Cumbres.

If any of the stock men failed to have their stock at the loading points, the entire schedule could be affected, and they might have to hold their stock until the schedule could be re-arranged.

STOCK SCHEDULE FOR 1935 SEASON

SOUTH SHEET

DATE	Order DRG	NO. RGS	SD.	DD.	Loading Point.	Destination.	SHIPPER.
9-23	538		3		Amargo	Denver	John Caranta
9-24							
9-25							
9-26							
9-27	460		5		Durango	Kansas City	W Dickerson
	547		7		Durango	Denver	R Frame
9-28							
9-29							
9-30							
10--1	302			38	Silverton	Denver	WL Thurston
	322	59		4	Glencoe	Denver	OE Schlegel
	323	60	10		Dolores	Kansas City	HR Holly
	496	119		4	Glencoe	Denver	Clem Honaker
	527	137		3	Hesperus	Denver	CC Harris
10--2	311			4	Silverton	Denver	JS Hartman
	298			8	Hooper	Denver	EP Hazzard
	439			2	Silverton	Denver	JC Thiery
10--3	259	34		10	Dolores	Denver	IW Brumley
	526	136	9		Dolores	Denver	Ed Manaugh
	546		6		Durango	Denver	Decker L & S
10--4							
10--5	293	50	16		Dolores	Kansas City	AH Bradfield
	328	65		3	Dolores	Denver	GA Meistrell
10--6	353	76	8		Dolores	Kansas City	King Bros
	396	91	3		Dolores	Kansas City	LL Stallings
10--7	370			6	Durango	Kans City	Sargent Long
10--8	505-128	15			Mancos	Denver	W Coppinger
	433-110			19	Hesperus	Kansas City	Long & Heather
10--9							
10-10	260	35	5		Dolores	Denver	W Veach
	292	49	9		Dolores	Denver	CM McCluer
	268			3	Durango	Denver	WA Short
	296			6	Durango	Denver	JW Jarvis
	340			10	Durango	Denver	Thompson & Townsend
	435	112	4		Glencoe	Denver	Raymond Ismay
10-11	245	21	7		Dolores	Kansas City	JA Morrison
	367			9	Amargo	Denver	CB McCoy
	379			12	Durango	Denver	CJ Petty
	466			8	Ignacio	Denver	A Jones
	477			5	Ignacio	Denver	JB Decker
	434	111		11	Dolores	Kansas City	Sargent Long
10-12	240			7	Rockwood	Gilcrest	OJ Carson
	244	20		10	Sheep Dolores	Kansas City	JA Morrison
	258	33		7	Dolores	Kansas City	EA Ritter
	273			28	Chama	Kansas City	E Sargent
10-13	313			18	Espanola	Kansas City	F Bond
10-14	271	40		7	Dolores	Denver	WR Veach
	274			28	Chama	Kansas City	Ed Sargent
	314			3	Chama	Kansas City	F Bond
	371			18	Ignacio	Kansas City	Sargent-Long
	375			12	Pagosa Jct	Kansas City	WF Kinderman
	528	138		4	Hesperus	Denver	WL Jaquez
	529	139	3		Dolores	Denver	James McCabe
10-15	380	94		15	Hesperus	Denver	JA Coppinger
	541	141		6	Mancos	Denver	Oen Noland
	550			10	Ignacio	Denver	HG Fulkerson
10-16	263			10	Servilleta	Mosca	A Graves
	272			30	Chama	Kansas City	TD Burns
10-17	321	58		3	Glencoe	Denver	RE Walker
	330			8	Durango	Denver	Guy Simmons
	372			10	Aztec	Kansas City	Sargent-Long
	395	90		3	Dolores	Kansas City	Homo Johnson
	398	93		7	Mancos	Denver	EA Ritter
	542	142	3		Dolores	Kansas City	Glen Majors
10-18	476			3	Durango	Denver	Tom Jaquez
	498	121		18	Dolores	Denver	MJ Adams
10-19	275			28	Chama	Kansas City	Ed Sargent
	544	144	15		Dolores	Denver	D Johnson
10-20	300	53		3	Glencoe	Denver	John Hinton
	339			4	Ignacio	Denver	AM Helton
	389			3	Durango	Denver	EF Sherman
	457			33	Chama	Kansas City	MA Gonzales
	502	125	12		Dolores	Kansas City	WR McCabe
	504	127		3	Glencoe	Denver	Grant Boyles
10-21	320	56		10	Glencoe	Denver	BM Barnard
	508	131		6	Glencoe	Denver	JL Byers
	509	132		6	Hesperus	Denver	Montoya Bros
10-22	279½			8	Dulce	Denver	R Sanchez
	301			9	Pagosa Jct	Denver	Gomez Bros
	321			5	Dulce	Denver	Gomez Bros
	361			7	Espanola	Denver	Merhege Bros
	511			4	Dulce	Denver	Jose G Garcia
10-23	376			10	Chama	Denver	WF Kinderman
	458			6	Chama	Kansas City	HC Moore
	315			19	Servilleta	Denver	F Bond
	280			14	Chama	Denver	Ed Sargent
10-24	303			40	Dulce	Denver	E Wirt
	382			10	Chama	Kansas City	Ed Sargent
	459			5	Dulce	Kansas City	Ed Sargent
	495	118	15		Dolores	Denver	IW Brumley
	543	143	5		Dolores	Kansas City	Ed Lockett
10-25	381			20	Chama	Kansas City	Ed Sargent
	417		15		Chama	Denver	Karsch Bros
10-26	314			18	Espanola	Kansas City	F Bond
10-27	316			5	Buckman	Kansas City	F Bond
	317			18	Espanola	Denver	F Bond
	359	82		7	Dolores	Denver	Jas Gawith
	373			5	Aztec	Kansas City	Sargent-Long
	374			14	Farmington	Kansas City	Sargent-Long
	415	101		13	Dolores	Denver	Tom Jones
	462			25	Farmington	Kansas City	Progressive Merc
10-28	499	122		11	Dolores	Denver	Floyd Adams
10-29	462			25	Farmington	Kansas City	Progressive Merc
	483			15	Chamita	Denver	Rueth & Cramer
10-30	464			25	Farmington	Kansas City	Progressive Merc
10-31	479			20	Farmington	Kansas City	Gallup Merc
11--1	465			25	Farmington	Kansas City	Progressive Merc
	416	102		13	Dolores	Denver	Bayless Sheep Co
	503	126	12		Dolores	Kansas City	WR McCabe

Colorado Railroad Musuem Collection, Robert W. Richardson Library

cars with roofs and lengthwise bench seating made from some of the steel underframe pipe cars.

One morning, while leaning against the fence opposite the engine, Foreman Lenny Winckel came along, and we idly chewed the fat. Glancing along the train, I voiced a question that had been in the back of my mind for some time: "How do you get away with mixing steel underframe cars with wooden ones?" A look of alarm spread over Lenny's face, not what I'd expected at all! The Rio Grande had forgotten all about the ICC ban on mixing steel and wooden passenger cars. Only a couple of years before a terrible casualty count resulted from such a mixture in Canada.

Lenny was greatly alarmed, and in musing over what to do, pointed out if the train, now about to depart, were delayed to switch cars, it would call attention to a lot of people best not made aware. Grimly he asked if I'd not say anything about this to anyone else, and we both agreed to keep quiet that day and just pray all went well.

Another time that morning, the train had the only operative engine at Durango, and there was some concern about what would be done if

Here are cabooses #0573 and #0587, as they appeared in March of 1948 when in use on the Silverton Mixed. The larger car was the regular car for crewmen, while the smaller car was assigned for sectionmen when they went along on winter trips. The #0573 was given for display along with Engine #223 to Pioneer Park in Utah and is now at the Ogden Railroad Museum. The #0587 was sold in 1966 to a park operation in Indiana and was destroyed in a fire. *Henry Bender*

At the Durango depot, the rear of the Silverton Mixed is on the track next to the station, while the *San Juan*'s consist is on the second track. Note that the end of the Railway Post Office car was reinforced with rails.

something went wrong on the trip—say the engine broke down, or a derailment occurred.

He said all he could do was expect to run the #490 he had warm, and despite it being banned as too heavy beyond Rockwood, he would ease it carefully around the high line at a crawl, but that the bridge was questionable.

He said he'd send one engineman to walk across the bridge, who would wait at the other end for the engine, after the fireman had slowly gotten it moving and then stepped off! Actually, he was certain the bridge wouldn't crumble despite its low rating.

One day when Foreman "Knucklejoint" Spearman was still in charge, he asked me if I could measure a curve. He had one he was certain was too sharp coming off where the loop started. I told him I couldn't use an instrument, but I did know how to use a knotted string to get the degrees of curvature.

His immediate instruction was to "go up town and get a ball of twine, I'll pay for it." So with a hostler holding one end of the string, we figured that curve took off at least 40 degrees! A #490 could carefully negotiate 26, but 40 was for streetcars, not 2-8-2s. Only later did I learn there'd been an ongoing dispute with the roadmaster, who insisted the curve was not excessive, so I pledged Knucklejoint to keep my name out of it,

Class K-36 #488, a 1925-built engine, is seen in service at Durango in the spring of 1953. It was sold to the new Cumbres & Toltec Scenic Railroad and is currently in use on that line. *Arthur W. Wallace*

as the track man was insisting the problem was with the engines, not with his switch.

Some of the railroaders who had homes at Alamosa would see me and come over and ask what was new or exciting back there, and so we would sort of exchange trivia information.

One day Foreman Winckel came up and asked how a railroad "nut" like me (being very tactful!) would know about tri cocks and water gauges and the like. So I told him my father was a steamfitter, and as a kid I had read at the Akron Public Library the ICC annual reports on boiler failures, etc., and that I had a great respect for care in tending boilers. He held out his hand and said, "Put her there!" and went on to tell me how the other morning they'd had quite a scare, and that my knowledge had helped avert real trouble.

A college student volunteer at the museum wanted to work on the Silverton that summer and had asked me who to see. He was lucky, as they needed a hostler helper, and he was hired. The night before driving to Durango he asked me what a hostler did, and did I have any information that might help him?

I told him of the three tri cocks on the engine boilers and the great importance in checking them and warned him not to rely on the reading in the gauge glass, and anyway to be sure to always blow down the gauge. I also reminded him I'd never been a hostler, and there were lots of things to learn, but those basics of the tri cocks and gauge readings were the most important.

It seems his very first morning on the job the night hostler had started good roaring fires in two engines due to be used that day. So "the kid" tried the middle cock on #476 and it just spit steam, so then he tried the bottom one, and it, too, spit steam instead of that reassuring flow of hot water that would have indicated the crown sheet was covered. In panic he ran for help, and fortunately the foreman was just coming in the door.

The #476 fire was dumped and the #490 was found in the same danger, although the gauge glasses in both engines showed plenty of

PANORAMA OF DURANGO, COLO.   X 1178

OPPOSITE LEFT. This black-painted diesel built by the U.S. Army was tried out at Durango and on the branches. It was designed to be used on various narrow gauges.

Here's a sweeping panorama of Durango. Looking to the north, the railroad facilities are at the bottom of the picture. The town was laid out by the D&RG with streets at right angles. Fort Lewis College sits atop the flat mesa at the right. The Animas River flows in the photo at top middle.

When movies were being made on the Narrow Gauge, visitors were startled by the strange appearance of some of the locomotives. The railroad no longer had any engines from the diamond stack and oil headlight period, so they equipped a more modern engine, such as this Mudhen (middle), for a movie. Here it is, ready to leave the Durango roundhouse. Note the large boxy headlight.

water. Apparently the departing sleepy night hostler hadn't tried any of the gauge cocks, nor had he blown down any of the gauges!

Neither engine was damaged. The crown sheets were very hot, but had not yet turned red. The foreman was amazed as he related to me when he quizzed the kid that a "rail nut" like me would know about such things. My stock went up, and he presented me that morning with a large carton, saying he had been going to burn the contents and then remembered me. The contents; many year's accumulation of cab cards for present and long-gone locomotives!

One morning while waiting for the Silverton to depart, I idly ran my eyes along the engine and tender, and I came alert when I noticed one vertical bolt in a tender archbar truck was up several inches and had obviously lost the double nuts normally found at the bottom of the bolt.

The engineer had oiled around and was now sitting in the cab waiting for the signal to go, so I went over and asked him when they quit double-nutting the archbar bolts. When I told him what I noticed, he

admitted he hadn't noticed it and called for the carman inspecting the train.

It was now train departure time, and of course, the crew gathered, and when the carman, a new man, temporarily replacing the regular man, came back from the roundhouse, the nuts he had were the wrong size.

So there was another long wait while he went back to get the right size plus another nut to replace one other the engineer had noticed missing on another truck. The Silverton went out about 40 minutes late that morning, but tender trucks received much more attention that summer!

The incident of the new hostler helper and the inaccurate water glass readings show how accidents can happen even when the oldest and most experienced employees are in charge.

That K-37 #490 2-8-2 had just come out of the Alamosa shop after an overhaul, and an engine crew of old heads had handled it on a freight to Chama, and another crew, also long-experienced, handled it on a freight to Durango.

A light engine runs east of Durango in this picture along the Animas River, which is unusual. It probably was being sent to the busy Farmington Branch during the "pipe boom" to help with switching. *Clayton Tanner*

Obviously the Alamosa shop people had overlooked the water glass spindles (there must have been something clogged), yet the two experienced engine crews reported nothing, as both engineers had "fiddled" with the tri cocks and ignored what the readings were in the water glass. Those old-timers could tell how much water they had and the steaming of the engine by using their ears and the tri cocks.

Jollification at Durango

I got up early one day in June 1954 and drove to Durango; it was just sort of an "abandoned lines reporter's" day of work. On the platform of the station was an odd scene, with various railroaders wearing the broadest smiles seen in those parts, and there was a general air of celebration.

In answer to my question if perhaps some consignee had declined a shipment of bourbon (they all seemed suspiciously happy), I was informed that word had just come over the wire "that blankety-blank is gone!"

What blankety-blank?

"Perlman!" came the answer.

Alfred E. Perlman had made himself no doubt the most hated person on the D&RGW. His ruthless methods to make the "bottom line look better" had certainly not endeared him to staff or employees; in fact there was an aura of fear among those people.

He always got good press, knowing how to turn on the charm to press people, but to those around and under him, a sharply critical sarcastic mood was often seen. In pursuit of the bottom line, and higher values for his stock options, he was pursuing a goal of scrapping as much of the line as possible. In a proper ICC writeoff, the narrow gauge lines were worth $30,000 a mile, a figure that had no bearing on additional scrap value or real estate. So the Alamosa-Durango line was worth $6 million! The 45-mile Silverton $1.25 million. And so on.

For his "hatchet man," he had named General Manager Kenneth L. Moriarty, a heavy drinker with a wonderful memory for names and the foibles of the various staff. K.L. had come up through the ranks, serving a training period at Gunnison. The two would visit a divisional office with one major goal, and that was "to cut." A committee was sent around the railroad to see what could be scrapped and what people could be fired.

The day after, the pair went on to the ruin of the New York Central with the two as president and general manager of that unfortunate line. D&RGW President McCarthy assembled all his department heads, and in a short lecture, informed them "this is no longer a one-man railroad," and that each department head from that day was expected to operate his section using his own judgment to the best advantage of the railroad.

Some things Perlman did were like those of other ruthless managers, and not very good policy. He decreed there would be no work trains unless authorized by himself personally and insisted that off-track machinery be used. Much more time was thus consumed in ditching and snow removing, things a Jordan spreader or drag flanger could do swiftly

ABOVE AND RIGHT. Built in 1881, #345 was moved to Durango from Gunnison in 1945 to become the yard engine. In making the movie *Denver & Rio Grande*, Engine #268 was the star, but the railroad did not want it wrecked in the head-on collision scene, so #345 was relettered as #268 and was the stand-in.

We see Class K-37 #499 at Durango. This engine was equipped year-round with a permanent plow pilot. It's now in reserve at the Cumbres & Toltec Scenic Railroad. *Clayton Tanner*

and without damaging track and roadway items. Doing ditching and snow removal with bulldozers and like machinery cost many ruined ties and other track damage.

Immediately after Perlman left, the roadmaster used the spreader for two weeks on the track west of Chama, declaring he had accomplished more in two weeks than in months of using off-track equipment, and with far less damage to ties.

What counted at the Denver office was that the records showed few work train miles. But poorer maintenance also had its dangers. One time a westbound freight near Toltec Gorge passed over a fill, at the bottom of which was a waterbox clogged with years accumulation of old leaves and other debris, which caused water to back up making quite a pond, which apparently softened the fill.

As the caboose rolled over that piece of track, the conductor, at his desk, felt the car sort of go down, and he staggered to the door just in time to get a glimpse of rails and ties seeming to be drooping on air! The fill had gone out! At Osier he gave a message to the section foreman.

A very bad tragedy was avoided. Waiting at Cumbres was a freight with two Helper engines to run ahead light. They, too, were warned. Because of the sharp curve approaching the fill, neither engine could have stopped in time! It took work trains two weeks to rebuild the fill and get a solid right-of-way again. The incident alerted employees to be on the watch for any other dangers due to neglect.

Restoring Ancient Style Domes on a Treasured Locomotive

When I bought narrow gauge Engine #346 in 1950, one noticeable difference between it and its sister Engine #345, the Durango yard switcher, was the incompleteness of the sand and steam domes. The #346 was missing most of its outer covering for both. Only the base rings remained on each dome.

They'd been complete when the engine was loaned with two sisters, #343 and #345, to the Colorado & Southern Ry. for use on the soon-to-be-abandoned South Park line. On July 25, 1936, the #346, running light down the eastern slope of Kenosha Pass, derailed on the first sharp curve and turned over in a swampy area. Engineer Eugene McGowan died the next day of injuries from scalding. Fireman W.S. Johnson jumped and received only minor injuries. An investigation determined the engine was being run too fast—fast in that area being anything over 12 mph.

At the time the Burlington had a big shop at Denver, and the C&S loaded the locomotive onto a standard gauge flat car, and sent it there to be restored. Most of the damage was cosmetic—as could be expected of 45 tons hitting a swamp! The top dome ring had been broken and discarded, and the Q fashioned a steam dome cover from one of the switch engines they were scrapping. Now of all the dozen C-19s of 1881 construction, only the #345 remained with those original distinctive ornamental as well as useful rings.

Then the film *Denver & Rio Grande* was made in the summer of 1951, and the #268 was brought from Gunnison to be the star locomotive. The plot called for a head-on collision of two trains, but the D&RGW needed the #268 for use at Gunnison, so #345 was selected to be its stand-in for the wreck.

In the movie are closeup scenes as the collision draws near, showing the #268 with its round "chocolate drop" modernized dome covers, and as the moment gets closer, there are cabside views past the obvious domes of #345, confusing to railfans and railroaders, but not to Hollywood. It was never clear if they noticed the difference or considered dummying covers for the #345's domes or the #268.

So #345, alias #268 and #319, collided with pyrotechnics Hollywood-style. Neither engine was seriously damaged, and the scene showed mostly black smoke. Towed afterward to the Durango yard, they were to be loaded onto heavy flat cars to go to Alamosa, thence by standard gauge to Pueblo to be scrapped.

To lighten the load, everything not needed on the engines was removed including rods, dome covers, etc., and quite a pile of scrap lay beside them. It was pointed out to me that there were the necessary rings to complete the #346. None had been damaged in the wreck.

Tom Cummins was road foreman and assistant to the Superintendent and was enthusiastic when I approached him about obtaining the parts for the domes. His first job had been as emergency fireman in 1909 on similarly-equipped engines on a stalled freight at Vance Junction on the Rio Grande Southern.

In his long career he had handled the throttle of the #346 and heartily approved my preserving it from scrapping. In a conversation with Roundhouse Foreman Newt J. "Knucklejoint" Spearman, it was decided not to attract attention in loading parts in my pickup. Newt said his wife was having a "hen party" that evening, and he usually walked down around midnight to check things at the roundhouse, and he'd meet me then and showed a rather winding trail to reach the scrap piles. "You be here then?" he asked.

It was a long ride back to Alamosa. I got so sleepy at Wolf Creek Pass that I pulled over and took an hour or so nap. Maybe longer. The sun was coming up when I reached home in south Alamosa.

The crews of passing trains always looked over to see what we were up to on our Mount Blanca & Western, so we figured we'd give them something new. We went to work. Those dome covers were like the old-time coal furnaces in homes, with the base casting into which a round sheet metal ring fitted, about 18 inches or so high, then the upper dome ring fitted onto that. Just a few bolts of no consequence and putting one together you could easily understand when a wreck or turnover occurred of an engine with those domes, the covers would fall off or break up.

About 10:30 a.m. when the two engines of Sunday's westbound freight slowly got under way and were passing the motel, the firemen and the head breakman were seen in the gangways. One fireman obviously was discussing the change in #346's appearance by pointing. Funny thing about all this was that when anyone mentioned the improved appear-

Oil headlights seldom survived wrecks. These specimens were found on Marshall Pass, relics of runaway trains of those early years before automatic air brakes.

This picture shows link and pin couplers for locomotives and cars. The coupler at left was standard for D&RG engines until replaced in 1903 by automatic couplers.

The classification lamps carried on the front of D&RG engines in the 1890s were termed "blizzard lamps." This one was so violently torn from the locomotive in a runaway wreck on Marshall Pass that the bracket holding the lamp was ripped from the engine. A small lever on the lamp enabled changing the colored glass to either red or green to show toward the front.

ance, they just assumed we had made the rings of wood! Noted car authority John Maxwell even complimented us on achieving such a "realistic" appearance. What could be more real than the real thing?

George C. Franklin and Perins Peak

One day, late in 1953, a tall, spry elderly man with blue eyes and a smile came into my office at Alamosa to inquire if he might see the exhibit that stated he had passed away.

He introduced himself as George C. Franklin, who in 1901 had opened the coal mine on Perins Peak, just outside Durango, the peak being a landmark that could be seen from Durango's Main Street.

Going through old files of the Rio Grande Southern, I had come across letters from the Boston Coal & Fuel Co. involving purchase of an engine from the RGS to be used on the five-mile narrow gauge line he was building to serve the coal mine. Although the junction point just outside Durango was named Franklin Junction, he declared it wasn't his doing.

We had opened up the new Narrow Gauge Museum in July of 1953 and among the frames was one with a letter signed by Franklin and various other items, including a photo of the train going to the driving of the silver spike ceremony on November 25, 1901. The engine was nicely painted and lettered for the coal company, and bore the name *Perins Peak* on the cab. The flat cars it was hauling were loaded with people bundled for the chilly day and seated on makeshift benches.

RGS Conductor Forest White noted in his daily record that they moved the flat cars with more than 250 people from Durango to the Junction, turning them over there to the BC&F crew, and picking the cars up again later in the day.

This sort of movement became a daily-except-Sunday affair as the mine went into production, except the "passengers" each morning were miners, as housing had not yet been built on the Peak. An employee timetable listed the BC&F train as a scheduled operation, indicating the BC&F engine and crew handled the train from the Durango yard.

Engine #1 was not only secondhand, it was really fourthhand! New in 1880, it came to the D&RG named *Chico*, one of a large number of Class 56 2-8-0 types. Six years later it was sold to the D&RGW Ry. (the Utah company, not the later 1921 company), and when the name changed, it became #79 of the Rio Grande Western Railway.

Then in 1891, with eight others of its class, it was sold to the new RGS and assigned the number 35. They first went to the D&RG shops at Burnham, Denver but #35 was still under repair when in July 1893 the Colorado world collapsed in financial ruin in what is termed the Crash of '93. The engine sat at Burnham until 1901 while the others meantime were sold to other roads, and thus in the guise of #1 Perins Peak, it finally made it to the RGS.

The Boston Coal & Fuel Co. became part of the D&RG-owned Calumet Fuel Co. in 1906, and the RGS took over operation of the branch. The #1 now became second #1 of the RGS. For several years it was largely kept in Perins Peak service, but also saw much service on the coal trains operated daily to the Hesperus and other mines. Most of the time operations on the branch required more than one train a day, as the mine was a big producer supplying much of the D&RG's needs, as well as the RGS.

Finally around 1911, the engine became very worn, and it was decided not to overhaul it but to take it to Ridgway for storage. This happened in 1913, and it was still there in 1926, stripped of many parts when it was scrapped. The long delay was because ownership and responsibility was in question, as it was owned by the Calumet Fuel Co.

After the coal company was sold in 1906, Franklin pursued his civil engineering work and was engaged by the Southern Pacific to handle allotting contracts for construction of that company's proposed railroad from the SP-owned coal lands near Durango to the Mexican port of Guaymas on the Pacific Coast.

He told of how he used a buckboard wagon, and the measurements were made by aid of a bucket of stones attached to the wagon wheels. So many turns of the wheel equaled so many yards, and subcontractors could go along and make their estimates at the same time.

The contractors gathered for a banquet at Gallup at which an announcement was to be made of the construction awards. But before this happened, a telegram arrived with word that E.H. Harriman, president,

Parlor-dinette car *Chama* was one of three such cars rebuilt in 1937 for use on the Alamosa-Durango passenger train. Inside were 10 individual deluxe seats. The attendant served meals throughout the day and also sold ice cream cones, etc. to people at wayside stops. One unique feature was an electrically-lighted tail sign for the named train *San Juan*.

had died and everything was put on hold. Harriman was pushing this construction against the advice of Vice President Julius Kruttschnitt. The latter permanently killed any work on the project.

The threat of this rival railroad, standard gauge at that, coming into the San Juan Basin led the D&RG to construct the standard gauge Farmington Branch in 1905, pre-empting the best route into Durango. Then in 1923, the D&RGW converted the branch to narrow gauge, and there was a little of the RGS involved as it was intended the first train would be using RGS #20, the famous ten-wheeler of later times. But, at the last minute, someone decided the initial train should have a locomotive lettered for the D&RGW.

Franklin was 85 at the time of his Alamosa visit. He'd had a long career in engineering projects, and in retirement at Del Norte, was author of various children's books.

The Passenger Fleet

When I moved to Alamosa in the fall of 1948, the D&RGW claimed to still have 32 passenger cars on its roster, to sustain a daily-each-way Alamosa–Durango 200-mile run, plus the once-or-twice-a-week Silverton Mixed. It was ample for the business.

All of the passenger cars were wood. Though only two mail and baggage cars were employed at a time, six of these cars were on hand. Four sat fading to a sickly light green in the "pickler" area (trackage at the west end of Alamosa yard which gained that odd name from the fact it had been used many years earlier by a lumber firm).

In summer, the five-car *San Juan* used a mail (RPO) and express car, baggage car, two of the vestibuled coaches and a parlor dinette. In winter, one coach was taken off, except during the Christmas holiday season, for about two weeks. The six vestibuled cars could seat but 24 each, as compared with the un-rebuilt four other open platform cars which had a capacity of 44.

The three parlor-dinette cars were named, instead of numbered, *Alamosa*, *Chama* and *Durango*. They carried color drumheads when in use, but having lost one drumhead in a misfortune earlier in 1948, one car always had a drumhead for the *Shavano*, the train that ran west out of Salida until 1940.

One last combination car, #212, was sufficient for the Silverton train, and the final car #313 *Silver Vista*, added to the summertime trains, was a glass-roofed affair with reserved seats. It had been an old coach in non-revenue service when rebuilt.

Primus Pearson, a car foreman, took a very personal interest in the appearance of the *San Juan* and each morning he was there to check the consist. He was known to have delayed departure to change out a car that he felt was not what it should be (i.e. exterior shiny Pullman green). He expressed regret that in the rebuilding of the RPO cars that the roof lines had not conformed to those of the other cars. To meet Post Office Department demands, those cars had a much higher clerestory roof than the other cars.

An open platform coach was kept at Durango in the event the Silverton's combine was insufficient, a rare happening other than in summer. A baggage car and another of the older coaches was kept at Gunnison, although never used. They'd been employed during WWII for some months when a highway bridge was out, so a two-car train made daily roundtrips from Gunnison to Montrose.

Actually there were only 31 cars, as one coach, #256, was a car body set off its trucks at Monarch, a wartime effort to provide carmen, stationed there in those times of gas rationing, with something of presumably the comforts of home. Gradually the car lost most of its crimson plush seats and was forgotten in car accounts until, during the 1950 hearings on discontinuing the *San Juan*, its presence at Monarch was noted. Officials rushed to Monarch to further dispose of the car, and especially its twin-bracket lamps.

Eventually, baggage #126 and coach #280 arrived in a monthly Valley Line freight, and the #280 was one of four open platform coaches remaining when the summer season of 1952 began on the Silverton, and it was given the Grande Gold paint scheme along with the other three, and combine #212.

The Silverton cars would come into Alamosa during the winter in freight trains, to be worked on by the carmen. But Denver was reluctant to put out money for repainting and would usually not budget the funds until the season opening was but weeks away. Then they would be sent west in a freight with crews instructed to watch for sliding wheels.

After the *San Juan* was discontinued in January of 1951, for several years the Rocky Mountain Railroad Club arranged to have a Memorial Day weekend excursion using 10 cars. All but one of the baggage cars had been scrapped, coach #280 was sent to Boulder for park display, and the #313 *Silver Vista*, which was used on some of the first trips, was destroyed by fire in 1954.

As the need for more seats on the Silverton became urgent, the car force removed the dinette and the 10 swivel chairs and restored the remaining parlor car *Alamosa* to a coach-seating format.

The Rocky Mountain Railroad Club sponsored pre-season trips on the narrow gauge from Alamosa to Silverton. Usually they required all of the remaining railroad's passenger cars.

Two

SILVERTON BEFORE THE TOURIST BOOM

My first trip on the Silverton Branch train was in the summer of 1941, during a vacation trip from Ohio. I had arrived on July 4th at Durango on the *San Juan* and was delighted to find that after six weeks of no trains due to spring high water and washouts, the mixed, Train 461, would operate the next day.

That morning there was a great deal of switching by old #346 to make up the train. Fifteen cars of sheep had arrived from Alamosa, and that with other freight, would require two locomotives. Watching the 1881 Consolidation do its work, I sure never had the faintest idea that some day I would own that locomotive.

Finally about 9:30 a.m. the train was ready. On the headend was #478, one of three remaining Class K-28 Mikados, still wearing the original spelled out roadname on the tender. Cut back behind the stock cars was Mudhen Class K-27 #459. The next year this engine was sent to Mexico and was so changed in appearance it would never be recognized as it sits today on a plinth in Mexico. Tailing the train was combination car #215 and the caboose.

Aside from sheepherders escorting their livestock loads, my friend and I were the only passengers. The crew was friendly, and Conductor Myron Henry even suggested we could ride the roof of the cupola if we wished, which was a wonderful spot to enjoy the scenery and train operations. It was also a place to quickly accumulate hot sparks, cinders and soot from the two engines, the prevailing breeze in the canyon heading for Durango, it seemed, at a much faster rate than the train progressed upgrade. I'd dressed for the occasion, but my friend had not and quickly abandoned the high perch to the somewhat more comfortable and cleaner interior of the combine.

Timetable rules limited speed of the mixed to 20 mph reducing it to 15 mph for sharp curves, so much of the trip was made at the latter gait. For the stretch of line around the High Line way above the river, the train simply crawled along at the 8 mph limit and observed carefully the injunction for the bridge at 5 mph. It was a fascinating trip with the long train of about 25 cars winding ahead, snow-covered peaks often in view.

The Animas River was mostly back in its banks, but it was still running swift and high from the snow melt. In

This is the #476 with the Silverton train at the station. It was a mixed train during the time before it became a popular tourist trip. *John Krause*

the valley just north of Durango the water had barely receded from the rails, and on the softened track the cars rocked badly.

When we reached Hunts there was a stop to assess the track. The roadmaster and sectionmen had gone out early to finish a shoofly track at this trouble spot. The crew told us of the many named spots, of which this was one. Their names were associated with persons who were present long ago or who had suffered some misfortune at the place. So Alexander Hunt, General Palmer's associate, was long remembered in this fashion, although no one could tell me why his name was attached to this trouble spot.

At this place slides would not only block the track with snow but so would a large amount of rock and dirt. The track was buried under a large mass of dirt and rocks so the shoofly was built around it, in the scant space remaining between the slide and the river.

The men needed a couple of carloads of fill, but didn't have time for that to be done, so the shoofly on a slight reverse curve dipped down several feet to cross the washed out area. Cautiously the train moved over this, everyone eyeing the car trucks and couplers, alert to give a stop signal if something went wrong. But all, engines and cars, negotiated it without difficulty. It was a typical piece of emergency trackage, I was told.

Several slide spots of the 30 or more pointed out to us were named for engineers who'd had trouble there, sometimes fatally. And along the way you could see now and then where the present grade deviated from some former location. The 45-mile trip was completed almost on the allotted timetable at three and a half hours.

Enroute at Tefft's Spur the sawmill location was pointed out where Otto Mears had ties cut. For many miles here and there we saw rails sticking out of the river or laying twisted along the banks, relics from long ago.

On arrival at Silverton, the cars of sheep were quickly spotted for unloading. The #459 tended to this while the #478 pulled the remainder of the train to the depot. Coming up that canyon with the wind blowing in my face, I headed for lunch uptown, while the crew spotted empties for concentrate loading and sorted out loaded box cars of concentrate.

On our return from lunch, the #459 was long gone, running light back to Durango. We planned to stay overnight and catch the bus the next noon for Montrose. This gave us time to explore the rather quiet town, obviously not fully inhabited, as smoke only issued from a few chimneys. It was obvious the best days of the mining industry were past.

At the Silverton Northern enginehouse a couple of blocks from the depot, vanadium ore from a nearby mine was being treated before shipment. The Silverton Northern Railroad 2-8-0 #4 and #3 had been moved a bit, and the tender of #4 had been uncoupled and moved outside. Beyond the end of D&RGW track I saw a couple of shabby box cars still lettered for the S.G. & N. R.R. (Silverton, Gladstone & Northerly). And another quarter mile further I saw the two-track enginehouse of that road. We couldn't see what was inside but were told by a passerby that the other engine (#34, an outside frame 2-8-0) and the passenger car

In a mistaken economy move, D&RGW management demolished the snowshed just four miles below Silverton. Even in mild winters serious slides occurred at this point. Here on March 31, 1949 #463 has left its train and is starting to buck the slide; as it came nearer the photographer it threw large chunks of frozen snow and ice high in the air. After just barely forcing its way through the slide, the engine went on another half mile to clear smaller slides, then backed down to get its train. In the final years of winter operations the mixed train tried to get through about every two weeks, postponing trips in bad weather.

SILVERTON BRANCH
Narrow Gauge

BRIEF DESCRIPTION OF LINE FROM PHYSICAL AND CONSTRUCTION STAND-POINT

Built Durango to Silverton in 1882, this line has a length of 45.61 miles. Route follows the Las Animas River throughout with the lower 15 miles in fairly open valley but subject to frequent floods and washouts. The upper 30 miles is in extremely rough and restricted canyon, with much of the line constructed on shelves and hillsides well above the river. There are numerous wooden bridges and trestles in this section over which speed restrictions prevail due to their obsolescence. There have been frequent interruptions to service on this line.

Grade is moderately heavy with a maximum of 2.5 percent. Alignment is fair on the lower portion but poor on the upper with numerous curves running to a maximum of 24 degrees.

Rail in place is approximately as follows:

Weight of Rail	Length		Date Laid
52#	6	miles	1911-1912
52#	4	"	1924
65#	22	"	1929-1930
85#	4	"	1929
90#	10	"	1940

This line is without special ballast other than natural gravel and fine rock developed in cuts during the construction.

ESTIMATED INVESTMENT COST TO DECEMBER 31, 1947
Val. Sec. Colo. 17-B   857,984.10

NORMAL MAINTENANCE ORGANIZATION

Section	-2 foremen with gangs of 1 man during Winter and up to 3 men during Summer for each section.
B&B	-1 gang averaging foreman and 6 men covers territory Chama to Durango and Silverton and Farmington branches.
Water Service	-1 pipefitter covers territory Chama to Durango and Silverton and Farmington branches.

THE DENVER AND RIO GRANDE WESTERN RAILROAD COMPANY
Statement of Revenues and Expenses
Silverton Branch - Years 1941 and 1948

SYSTEM REVENUES

Freight	1941	1948
Forwarded	$ 78,191	$ 123,786
Received	32,667	31,530
Total Freight	$ 110,858	$ 155,316
Passenger		
Passenger	$ 665	$ 6,065
Mail	484	432
Express	304	75
Miscellaneous	23	139
Total Passenger	$ 1,476	$ 6,711
Total System	$ 112,334	$ 162,027

BRANCH LINE

*Freight Revenues		
Forwarded	$ 19,644	$ 31,560
Received	11,230	13,738
Paid R.G.M. Way	Dr 698	Dr 1,149
Total Freight	$ 30,176	$ 44,149
Passenger Revenues		
Passenger	$ 665	$ 6,065
Mail	484	432
Express	304	75
Miscellaneous	23	139
Total Passenger	$ 1,476	$ 6,711
Total Branch Line Proportion	$ 31,652	$ 50,860
Expenses		
Maintenance of Way and Structures	$ 15,907	$ 27,750
Maintenance of Equipment	3,070	7,198
Transportation Expenses	13,933	30,126
Total Expenses	$ 32,910	$ 65,074
Net Operating Revenue	D$ 1,258	D$ 14,214

*Based on Revenue Ton Mile Prorate with Minimum 25%

D- Donotes Deficit

Silverton Branch - Continued

BALANCE OF RAILROAD

	Basis I Expenses Computed on 50% Operating Ratio		Basis II "Out-of-Pocket" Expenses	Basis III "Full Operating" Expenses
	Year		Year	Year
	1941	1948	1948	1948
Revenues	$ 80,682	$ 111,167	$ 111,167	$ 111,167
Expenses	40,341	55,584	92,577	113,772
Net Operating Revenue	$ 40,341	$ 55,583	$ 18,590	D$ 2,605

TOTAL EARNINGS VALUE TO SYSTEM

Total System Net Earnings Adjusted	$39,093	$ 41,369	$ 4,376	D$ 16,819
Adjusted Total System Net Earnings (1)	--	$ 38,778	D$ 2,277	D$ 32,769
Estimated Total System Net Earnings After Allowing for Adjustment and Taxes	--	D$ 6,794	D$ 47,849	D$ 78,341

D- Denotes Deficit.

(1) Adjusted to allow for increased freight rates and wage rates- 1949 over 1948.

Capital Expenditures	1941	1948
Road - Gross	$ 1,368	Cr $ 64
Road - Net	Cr $ 10,914	Cr $ 159

Taxes		
Ad Valorem	$ 29,813	$ 45,572

Statistics of Train Operation		
Number of Trains Operated	206	180
Train Miles	9,284	8,016
Gross Ton Miles (1000)	2,067	2,249
Net Ton Miles (1000)	924	947
Average Net Tons per Train	100	118
Average Net Tons per Day (306 Days per Year)	67	69

Basis I- Based on formula used in abandonment proceedings before the ICC.
Basis II- Based on out-of-pocket expenses, i.e., those that tend to vary with the train miles and car miles operated, including locomotive repairs, car rental (inc. repairs), fuel, trainmen and enginemen wages, water-lubricants-supplies for locomotives, enginehouse expense, transfer cost, and switching.
Basis III- Based on a gross ton mile proportion of full operating costs for M of W&S, M of E, and Transportation, as shown in the Income Account, excluding deferred Maintenance Credits.
Note: Year 1941 expenses not computed under Basis II and Basis III account necessary traffic flow data not available.

Budget and Statistics,
November 23, 1949

THE DENVER AND RIO GRANDE WESTERN RAILROAD COMPANY

Silverton Branch Station Earnings Freight and Passenger Years 1934 to 1948 Inclusive

Year	Amount	Year	Amount	Year	Amount
1934	$ 103,840	1939	$ 91,368	1944	$ 106,144
1935	94,057	1940	118,315	1945	104,639
1936	135,365	1941	111,159	1946	176,111
1937	184,604	1942	96,087	1947	212,928
1938	235,143	1943	103,169	1948	155,882

	1941				1948			
	Freight For'd	Freight Rec'd	Passgr For'd	Total	Freight For'd	Freight Rec'd	Passgr For'd	Total
Animas City	$ 3	$	$	3	$	$	$	
Hermosa						2	1	3
Rockwood	105		23	128	536	382	60	978
Tacoma	1	126		127	64	249	27	340
Tefft		14	14			4	36	40
Needleton		26	26					
Elk Park		119	119					
Hunt						8		8
Silverton	78,085	32,379	278	110,742	123,184	30,886	443	154,513
Total	$78,191	$32,667	$ 301	$111,159	$123,786	$31,530	$566	$155,882

Branch Line Proportion- Minimum 25%								
	$19,644	$11,230		$ 30,874	$31,560	$13,738		$ 45,298
Paid RGMW		698						1,149
				$ 30,176				$ 44,149
Passenger (In and Out)		665						6,065
Mail		484						432
Express		304						75
Miscellaneous		23						139

Total Branch Line		$31,652						$ 50,860

*Includes Silver Vista car revenue

Freight Accounting Department,
June 27, 1949

THE DENVER AND RIO GRANDE WESTERN RAILROAD COMPANY

Commodities Handled On the Silverton Branch
Years 1941 and 1948

Commodities	1941			1948		
	Cars	Tons	Revenue (System)	Cars	Tons	Revenue (System)
Local Freight Originated At And Destined to Points On The Branch						
Manufactures & Miscellaneous	1	5	$14			
All LCL Freight			14	12		$ 162
Total	1	5	$28	12		$ 162

Freight Moved From Branch Points To System Points
And To Branch Points From System Points

Commodities	Cars	Tons	Revenue	Cars	Tons	Revenue
Flour, Wheat	1	10	$ 32			$
Flour, Edible, NOS	1	15	52			
Hay	6	40	144	14	85	388
Horses, Mules, Ponies & Asses				4	38	107
Cattle & Calves, SD				6	60	126
Sheep & Goats, SD	8	59	189	25	197	948
Sheep & Goats, DD	69	613	925	128	1,280	3,021
Bituminous Coal	125	2,965	3,240	120	2,919	4,306
Iron Ore	24	796	5,997			
Lead Ore & Concentrates	69	2,592	13,748	101	5,104	65,674
Ores & Concentrates	183	6,466	44,182	56	2,441	17,366
Fluxing Stone & Raw Dolomite				1	49	578
Posts, Poles & Piling	2	23	123			
Lumber, Shingles & Lath	2	22	67	1	20	96
Gasoline	7	150	542			
Lubricating Oils & Greases				3	26	128
Chemicals, NOS				2	11	53
Manufactured Iron & Steel	1	7	126			
Iron & Steel Pipe & Ftgs, NOS				1	18	497
Machinery Parts	4	56	1,109	1	11	186
Ammunition & Explosives	19	205	4,142	20	148	4,325
Cement: Natural & Portland				6	98	1,126
Scrap Iron & Steel	6	177	1,200	1	38	336
Waste Material for Remelting NOS				3	147	1,738
Manufactures & Miscel. NOS	34	560	3,460	4	36	105
All LCL Freight		480	9,431		168	3,754
Total	561	15,236	$88,709	497	12,894	$104,858

Freight Accounting Department,
June 27, 1949

Commodities	1941			1948		
	Cars	Tons	Revenue (System)	Cars	Tons	Revenue (System)

Freight Moved From Branch Points To Points On Other Roads
And To Branch Points From Other Roads

Commodities	Cars	Tons	Revenue	Cars	Tons	Revenue
Sheep & Goats, DD	45	355	$ 748	14	142	$ 1,566
Bituminous Coal				1	24	34
Lead Ore & Concentrates				1	51	495
Zinc Ore & Concentrates	43	1,696	9,073	80	3,895	30,087
Ores & Concentrates, NOS	5	206	1,103			
Products of Mines, NOS	2	33	307			
Lumber, Shingles & Lath	28	455	4,123	6	99	1,284
Gasoline	1	23	247			
Fuel, Road & Pet. Residual Oils, NOS				1	20	267
Lubricating Oils & Greases	2	15	160			
Chemicals, NOS				4	70	1,631
Sodium (Soda) Products				3	51	1,341
Fertilizers, NOS				2	30	320
Manufactured Iron & Steel				1	10	201
Iron & Steel Pipe & Ftgs., NOS				1	20	301
Machinery Parts	18	334	3,315	16	233	3,307
Cement, Natural & Portland				2	31	580
Lime, NOS				5	65	643
Scrap Iron & Steel	9	226	1,253	10	409	3,616
Waste Materials for Remelting NOS				1	49	740
Manufactures & Miscel. NOS				3	43	1,154
All LCL Freight		64	1,764		71	2,567
Total	153	3,407	$22,093	151	5,313	$50,134
Grand Total	715	18,648	$110,830	648	18,219	$155,154

Freight Accounting Department,
June 27, 1949

Colorado Railroad Museum Archives

A southbound mixed train on the Silverton Branch rounds the High Line in the 1950s, where the track is about 270 feet above the Animas River. *Clayton Tanner*

were inside. Outside was a weary looking flanger car and caboose. A very rusty main line of the Silverton Northern could be seen winding out of town, heading for Eureka where a mine still functioned, but whose output was trucked to Silverton for loading.

At Silverton they liked to say they never had summer, just a late spring and early fall, and it sure seemed that way that night, for despite it being July, the water trickling down the unpaved streets froze, and we two seemed to just about do the same in the unheated hotel. The only heat in the building was what might trickle out of the owner's kitchen.

Ice water in the bathroom was not very effective in washing my sooty, tear-streaked face, and I had to wait until we got to Grand Junction the next evening to achieve the luxury of hot water for that purpose.

The Silverton Branch in 1941 was not yet the tourist attraction it was to become. The twice-a-week train, if it ran, carried the combination car which was ample for the business. A few people rode the train; the only alternative was a daily Rio Grande Motorways bus, but the crew said most of the time they had at best maybe two or three passengers, and often none at all.

The mixed train of the Silverton tried to reach the town on February 5, 1951 but was forced to back to Rockwood, as after clearing several rocks and small slides, it encountered a huge slide at the site of the former snowshed. It was to take two more trips, the final one using #463 and a huge pilot plow, to reach Silverton.

OPPOSITE LEFT. This is a typical scene in the spring and early summer on the Silverton Branch. High water has cut into the main track, so the sectionmen have completed a shoo-fly at the site. The branch had many sites where over the years the track had been slightly relocated due to high water and snowslides.

The next year the D&RGW also sold some passenger cars to the National of Mexico including the combination car #215, but the former #215 still runs on the branch, thanks to some juggling of car bodies. Mexico actually got #212, and the body of #215 was renumbered to #212. The evidence was clear for years by the blanked out clerestory portion where #215 had a cupola when it was used on the long-gone Pagosa Springs Branch.

The three locomotives at Silverton went to the White Pass & Yukon during WWII, and, of course, did not return. They were hauled dead to Alamosa Shop, overhauled and tested, before shipment from Seattle. The remaining track of the roads at Silverton was scrapped in 1942, used as steel for the war effort. One of the SG&N box car bodies was converted to

a warehouse by the local oil company outlet, and if you were to crouch underneath it you could see the maze of piping which equipped the car to use straight as well as automatic air brakes.

Silverton Branch Problems

The 30 miles of canyon on the Silverton Branch posed constant problems, endangering its survival after the end of mining traffic. Those of us who wanted the line to survive worried that whoever might buy it would not be able to financially overcome the problems.

In winter there were often large avalanches, bringing not only vast amounts of snow onto the tracks, but rocks and trees as well. And if there were heavy snows during a winter, this inevitably meant high spring runoff washouts. In summer the frequent scattered showers could turn into a cloudburst with danger to the tracks but also the possibility of stranding hundreds of passengers.

As if this were not enough discouragement in a dry summer, there was danger from sparks starting not just little brush fires, but raging forest fires sweeping up the canyon sides. The Forest Service, watching its rapidly depleting budget, had sought to collect for its costs, and the past several years has seen claims of several hundred thousand dollars for train-ignited fires.

Engine #463 with a short mixed train brings some very welcome cars of coal to isolated Silverton in 1951. The combine carried but two passengers on this trip.

40

Equipped with the huge snowplow, the #463 handles the mixed for Silverton on the High Line. Although there wasn't any snow on the first portion of the trip, eventually the engine had to buck through slides higher than the stack.

Standard equipment in my G-buster carryall was a long-handled shovel and a broom or two. They were very handy to put out small blazes when chasing some train working up Cumbres or Dallas Divide. It was not enough, for a blaze started near Toltec Gorge by careless picnickers, and the Forest Service had to use a tanker to quench a huge smoldering fallen tree.

Naturally, riding the Silverton, I had neither my trusty shovel or broom, two items passengers don't carry. So one summer day I chose to ride the narrow platform of the *Silver Vista*, and Conductor Myron Henry asked if

A snowplow-affixed K-27 #463, with a mixed train, arrives in snow-covered Silverton after battling snow and snowslides on March 31, 1953. There's only one coach on this train—more passengers will come later. *Robert W. Richardson, collection of Mallory Hope Ferrell*

I was intending to stay there, and if so, would I watch out for fires, and if sighted one blazing behind the train, to slowly open the air valve and stop the train. Often the sectionmen following the train would be so busy with one blaze that another could gain size before they could get to it.

A couple miles later, all of a sudden several hundred feet behind the train a clump of bushes burst into high flames and there was no sign of the sectionmen, so I slowly opened the valve, and the train came to a stop with the protesting #476 up ahead giving some last sharp stack noise.

Myron evidently forgot to mention me to his brakemen, who went along the train looking for an ailing air hose or whatever, and when he rounded the end of the *Silver Vista*, a lady who hadn't been there to hear Myron's instructions, pointed at me as the culprit, shrilly exclaiming, "He did it—I saw him turn that valve!" So I had to explain to the brakeman, and meantime the sectionmen had reached the fire, and just about had it out so we didn't have to go to their aid.

But sometimes it took a concerted effort to put out a blaze as the movie people learned. During filming of *Denver & Rio Grande* in 1951, actors, extras and workers all had to abandon their roles and jobs to grab tools and brooms to put out fires, much to the detriment of the director's schedule. They were using three locomotives during filming, and some days there was very little filming accomplished. Sometimes they were lucky, and if the fire was on the same side as the blowoff valve of the engine, a quick pass with the valve held open put out a fire in seconds.

Worries about the Silverton

In the early 1950s, Al Perlman let it be known that the D&RGW would sell the Silverton Branch, and various people with no railroad operating experience and usually with no money either, expressed their desire to take over.

Aside from those feelings, was the worrisome fact that whoever took it over ought to be able to finance expensive restoration should the inevitable spring high water or cloudbursts damage the line. No financially responsible buyers turned up. There was considerable outrage when the Thatcher banking family interests made a move to purchase the line, and after some time, they withdrew.

Confusing the whole matter were the plentiful sharp characters, not to mention downright dishonest ones, of which Colorado always seemed to have many among its permanent and transient population.

The railroad management quietly promised Walter Knott of Knott's Berry Farm the engines and rolling stock for his Calico Desert he was planning. After the Brinkerhoff brothers completed tearing up the Gunnison line in 1955, they were advised to hang onto their equipment, as soon the Silverton Branch would be available for their skills. As a railroad has no such things as secrets, all of these became common knowledge.

FOLLOWING PAGE. Rio Grande Southern Engine #42 (ex-Class C-17 D&RG #420) awaits its end as scrap, having completed its work in the dismantler's train in March of 1953. It was sold for preservation the next month to Robert W. Richardson. After being displayed at Alamosa until 1958, it was then sold to Magic Mountain for their park near Golden, Colorado. Eventually the Durango & Silverton Railroad bought it, and it is now displayed in their Durango museum. *Arthur W. Wallace*

In 1950 when the Silverton was equipped with Engine #473 and four cars painted Grande Gold, I produced this postcard, the first one of the Silverton, and tried to get a few outlets to stock it to publicize the train. The effort was not a great success and less than 500 were made. Today postcard dealers offer them for $12!

ENGINE OF THE "SILVERTON"
- SOUTHWESTERN COLORADO -
"NARROW GAUGE COUNTRY"

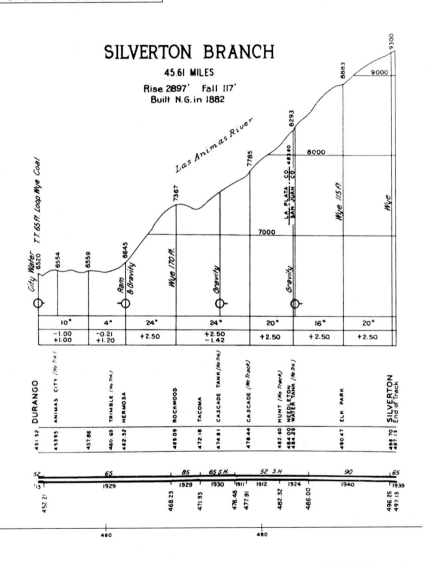

SILVERTON BRANCH

45.61 MILES

Rise 2897' Fall 117'
Built N.G. in 1882

In the spring of 1953, 1903 Mudhen Class K-27 #452 awaits forwarding to Alamosa for dismantling. The engine had last been used on loan to the Rio Grande Southern in November of 1951. *Arthur W. Wallace*

ABOVE AND RIGHT. This was a costly accident for the Silverton train when Engine #473 was derailed due to a sun-kinked rail. The engine all but turned over on a pile of rocks. The re-railing was accomplished without a crane by using jacks and blocks to literally build a track under the locomotive.

Rio Grande Land, Resurrection of the 'Silverton'

"We have a little gold mine on our hands and don't know what to do with it," said D&RGW Passenger Traffic Manager Harold F. Eno in an unguarded moment at an off-line traffic meeting with others of his rank from various Midwestern roads.

It was a harsh truth, as each summer in the 1950s there were more and more passengers showing up, or rather would-be passengers, which the 10 items of rolling stock couldn't accommodate.

Management's view was expressed by one official when visiting Alamosa that "hauling people on a sightseeing roundtrip to Silverton is neither public necessity nor public convenience," and that when they were ready to apply to abandon the branch, the Interstate Commerce Commission would agree and approve it.

"So," he told me, "you are wasting your time in advertising the train as a tourist attraction." When one year somehow it got to the press that the train had netted $93,000, another angry railroad official declared that there was such small change in the railroad passenger business that he "wouldn't stoop to pick it off the floor."

And meantime the road's public relations director, a Durango-raised youth before he worked for the railroad, sarcastically declared that "only railroad nuts like you" would ride something like the Silverton. It turned out he thought all the growing passenger totals were railfans and was astounded to learn that likely less than 4 or 5% were railfans, and that

the rest were tourists. He couldn't believe that tourists, frequently entire families, took the train.

So it wasn't surprising that in 1959 the road formally applied to the ICC to abandon the line, citing the almost total loss of freight traffic, the last large mining shipper closing down in 1953, and no indications of any mining revival in the area.

The real surprise came on April 23, 1962, a day that should be annually commemorated in Durango and Silverton. The commissioners issued their findings, denying the application, and citing the present and future prosperity of the line in profitably hauling tourists.

In the 1960s it was indeed unusual, if not unique, that a mixed train with little freight was turning in an increasing amount of revenue and profit.

Early in 1963 came startling news. Management had reversed itself in regards to the train and was ready to improve it in many ways. Alexis McKinney, who had been assistant for years to the publisher of the *Denver Post*, and more recently handled public relations for the D&RGW, was appointed director of what was now termed "Rio Grande Land."

Not being a railroader, he brought many new ideas to the operation, most of which were adopted. Not being a railroader, he wasn't hampered by years of things having to be done "by the book." With diplomatic skills he managed the problems of unions, contracts and their often hard-to-believe agreements on so many small items.

At Denver two new coaches were built early in the year. Being made of steel, they would resemble the older cars, even having scribed sides to imitate wooden siding. Steel passenger trucks were obtained from the last two RPO cars. The baggage car was changed to a snack car. Business car B-7 was also sent to Denver to acquire Grande Gold paint and be readied for use as a chartered car for $150 per trip.

The two new cars increased capacity of a train to near 500, but still at the height of the season people were turned away. It was announced that three days a week a second train would be operated. With a dry track, one K-28 could manage, with hard work in some places, to handle 12 cars.

There was a need for an open car of some kind, and pipe gondola #9605 was requisitioned to add to the train. At times conductors had been using just any gondola that could be cleaned up somewhat. So two more gondolas were added, these being supplied with their former standard gauge box car roofs, a welcome addition on a trip that often encountered showers.

At Durango the winter of 1962–63 buzzed with rumors about the area, that someone was buying up real estate near the depot. During a January 10 meeting, railroad representatives announced that the entire block from the depot up Main Street had been purchased by the railroad, with the intent to upgrade the two old hotels and make other properties available to preferably local business interests to tie in with train operations.

Coach #327 was a rebuild of an open platform coach of 1887, and used on the *San Juan.* Afterwards it was employed on the present Silverton train. *Clayton Tanner*

Upgrading of the track was undertaken, first in the meadows just north of Durango where the track was often rather soft in spring and subject to flooding by an out-of-its-banks Animas River. On one trip in the 1950s there was water several inches over the rails, and the cars rocked ominously on the uneven rails on dirt ballast.

Up around Needleton was the lightest rail on the branch, some of it worn out 56-pound and similar second- and thirdhand rail, and these were replaced with other heavier, secondhand rails and hundreds of new ties. Carloads of track material were often seen heading out of Alamosa for the branch.

On July 6, 1963 the first of the second sections was operated. The scheduled train used the numbers of the long-time mixed, #461 and #462. For many years nothing out of Durango had needed green flags on the first section to indicate another section was following. Trainmaster Meek, who always ended up with the operating problems, bought some green cloth at a store, and Roundhouse Foreman Leonard Winckel's wife sewed the flags on her home sewing machine.

That pair of flags was used many times that summer. Proudly it was reported that on July 25 the passenger total for the two sections went over 600. The use of walkie-talkies speeded up loading and reduced delayed departures by trainmen checking the cars for empty seats so that everyone possible could be taken along.

The upstairs office space that for years had been the lonely headquarters of the Rio Grande Southern was overhauled, and now when someone reached the head of the stairs a secretary met the visitor. The former baggage room was rebuilt with large restrooms; the express area became a waiting room. No longer was the ticket agent also the telegrapher, and many other chores were given to someone else. Now, waiting was reduced by adding more ticket windows and swifter handling of reservations.

One costly problem was the maintenance of a yard engine and crew of switchmen who now had very little to do. Freight service had declined by the 1960s, and by 1964 only one freight a week might show up at Durango. The yard crew had only a little switching some mornings and had to turn the trains on arrival in the evening.

At Baker, Oregon, a lumber firm had three-rail trackage in its yard, vestiges of the long-gone Sumpter Valley Railway, and to do in-plant switching they'd been using a small four-wheel Davenport-Besler. Purchased in the fall of 1963 by the D&RGW, the 30-ton growler was tested with a string of freight cars to see if it could handle the switching. The passenger cars were at Alamosa for the winter, and thus ended use of a steam locomotive for Durango switching. In the last 80 years, just about every class of locomotive has sufficed as switchers, commencing in the 1890s with otherwise surplus 4-4-0 types.

One day the Alamosa westbound freight included a box car, bright in Grande Gold. The car force had turned out #3219 at the request of McKinney so that when the train had some mountain climbers or camp-

ing parties, and their baggage, they could travel in style right behind the engine.

Also rolling west for the spring opening was remodeled combination car #212, now a snack car for the second sections which, however, were now timetable numbers #463 and #464, and the green flags dirty and cinder-burnt, lay idle in Meek's office.

There were smiles not only in Denver, but around the country, when the annual report stated the branch had earned $18.11 per train mile. The railroad industry by 1964 had about given up on profits from passengers, and this kind of news from Colorado must have had many a traffic manager looking wistfully at his red-ink streamliners.

Six more steel coaches were authorized in 1963–64, and for the first time that summer the train ran daily, the second train commencing in July. The season was June 3 through September 30. Switching and loading and unloading at Silverton was eased by adding a second track ending within a block of the main street.

A national strike was called the evening of July 11; that same day the second track was first used, and local members of the Brotherhood of Locomotive Firemen & Engineers went out, too. It was July 12 and the height of tourist season and to not run a train was unthinkable. So with various officials, like the roundhouse foreman at the throttle and even McKinney serving as a brakeman, the train made the run. Meanwhile, the strike was called off just after the train departed.

In the 1950s as passenger business boomed on the Silverton train, the tracks at Silverton were extended a short distance so that passengers could disembark only a block from the main street. Kendall Mountain looms in the rear.

The year 1964 ended with a passenger total of 65,177 for the season, a figure that made me smile, recalling a Rio Grande official years before on an excursion, tapping me on the chest and pronouncing that "no one except camera nuts like you would pay to ride this junk" sweeping his arm to include the interior of one of the vestibuled coaches. The year also saw business car B-2 return from that back yard in Oklahoma to be available for charter parties, people who didn't seem at all inclined to view their quarters as "junk."

With so much accomplished and things running smoothly, McKinney, with feelings of mixed pleasure and weariness at "running a railroad," accepted the post of Public Relations Department head on May 1, 1965, in Denver. His last gesture in his traffic position was arranging for purchase of three buses so that more passengers could be handled by those riding the train in one direction. This pleased thousands who didn't want to spend the entire day on trains.

Sale of the Silverton

D&RGW officials expected that once the line east of Durango was gone, they could abandon the Silverton Branch at their pleasure. One official told me that the Interstate Commerce Commission would not consider the "hauling of sightseers on a roundtrip to Silverton" as the determining rule of "public necessity and convenience." But the railroad waited too long, and they found out they were wrong.

Eventually the D&RGW decided that running a tourist train was not really what they wanted to do, and were quite pleased finally, after various false starts, to sell the branch to a Florida citrus grower, Charles E. Bradshaw, in 1981.

Bradshaw had no previous experience in running a railroad, but he had some good ideas on how to make it profitable and satisfy the general public—and at the same time pay off his debts associated with improving the property.

His first day was what I call "a sudden swoop." He changed all locks, the property was promptly fenced, and a security force sometimes referred to as his "coal and iron police" patrolled the Durango yard. Except at train times, access to the track side of the station was denied.

This was not taken kindly by many, but it had a very practical purpose. Ever since the number of passengers had increased, the problem at the roundhouse and yard was that passengers who visited the roundhouse wandered around, spending too much time talking with employees.

In the Perlman and Moriarty administration the D&RGW tried to stop this by ordering employees to escort such visitors off the property. The payroll costs of chatting were not inconsiderable. For a few days the employees tried to enforce the order, but had to give up, as now they were spending even more time with the passengers, some quite irate. One memorable morning a New England photographer was seen being literally carried by two roundhouse employees up to the street, tripod and all!

Rebuilding Passenger Cars

Bradshaw put skilled men to work, completely rebuilding old retired passenger cars that had been in work service, with every bit of rotten wood being replaced.

The old woodbeam passenger trucks were suspect, and very expensive to maintain, so new steel trucks, at a cost of $10,000 each, were manufactured by an outside firm. All the new cars, or rather new-old cars, were given appropriate names as well as numbers. Even old #311, the duck-billed roof car that had been sold to the Montezuma Lumber Co. and had become a home, was eventually seen in the consists.

Bob Shank, Jr. had started accumulating some items in his short-lived Narrow Gauge Museum just north of town near Hermosa. He'd resurrected the #311, and converted some old woodbeam Burlington Route caboose trucks for it, and for a while the car rode to Silverton on those!

More open cars were built for the Silverton Branch, and eventually there were more than 40 cars available for the trains. The three private cars were purchased from their owners and became special charter party operations, the former B-3 *Nomad* being the star of the group.

The track received extensive work. It was reballasted, and replacement rail was installed. Over the years the Rio Grande upgraded the rail, but had never done such extensive ballasting. When this work was completed the trains ran smoothly, without the rocking that had become normal during the D&RGW's tenure. Extensive work was done to crib the High Line, where on sharp curves the track was several hundred feet above the Animas River.

Finding Motive Power

At first, for motive power, there were only the three remaining K-28 2-8-2s, all Alco-produced products of 1923. The D&RGW had left #481 and #497 (Classes K-36 and K-37) at Durango, but until the track was upgraded, and the High Line completely rebuilt, the two larger engines could not be used.

Eventually #493 and #499 were brought by truck from the remnants of the Alamosa roundhouse, but the K-37 just did not perform well on the tight curves of the Silverton. After years of effort, in the spring of 1999, the #499 was traded for the #486 on display at the Royal Gorge. Other #490s had gone in trades to the Cumbres & Toltec Scenic RR.

A shop was built and equipped with machinery so that most any work required could be done at Durango, and it could also help to pay its way by taking in custom work from elsewhere. They hadn't intended to build a new roundhouse, but in 1990 the building was engulfed in flames, trapping some engines. It was rebuilt much better than the original and enlarged, and what remained of the old roundhouse became storage. Under the new owners of 1998 that portion became a very fine museum.

A motor car and trailer were built to use especially on shorter roundtrips to Cascade. A depot was placed at Rockwood, which was a former RPO car, but the effort was not much of a success. Despite the

The Silverton train followed the canyon of the Animas, most of the time only a few feet above normal water levels. Consequently, many times a heavy spring freshet or a summertime cloudburst washed out trackage. But most of the track was on a rock base, and repairs usually only took a short time. Some early floods wrecked tracks for miles, and the rails from those events are still seen lying in the Animas River.

nicely-designed open trailer, many people didn't want to drive the 15 miles to Rockwood from Durango.

Some estimated that all told, Bradshaw had invested $5 million in the Silverton, including his purchase price of $2.2 million. It was not long before four trains a day operated in the height of the summer season.

The ticket office was efficiently operated under the direction of Amos Cordova, former agent-telegrapher at various D&RGW points. And eventually, the line was handling just over 200,000 passengers a year, not bad at all for a trip scorned by a former D&RGW official who declared "only you rail nuts will ride a thing like that."

Some things didn't work out so well. Most of the D&RGW employees were at retirement age and took it. So one year the trainmaster, a former D&RGW man, solved the enginemen shortage by in his own words, hiring "a group of good old Rio Grande men."

These were diesel men, currently laid off at Grand Junction during a low period of traffic. Well skilled in handling long freights on the main line with modern power, they hadn't any experience with steam locomotives.

At the station during the waiting-to-depart period, they were never seen down on the ground oiling around, but instead sat in the cab waiting for the signal to go—after all, oil cans were not employed around diesels. They started up with the reverse lever low in the corner, and not knowing any better, left it there, so the train would amble up the fairly level easy stretch along the highway north of town. It was the equivalent of driving your car in low gear!

The newly-appointed firemen also were unfamiliar with steam. They would get off their seat and shovel in 11 to 14 scoops of coal, which of course, mostly went out the stack in a big cloud of smoke that lowered visibility on the adjacent busy highway. Four, maybe five scoops was good firing.

I watched one former engineman shout in rage at the passing train (although, of course, the engine crew couldn't hear him), at this abuse of the locomotives. There was quite a bit of work to be done on the engines that winter.

Passengers commented on the smoky runs, not just on the continuous grades to Silverton, but also all the way back, mostly downgrade! The quality of fuel was good, as was true most of the time during D&RGW's reign.

Experience counts. New employees, some never having ridden any kind of train before, had to be educated on the use of handbrakes, and the brake club. Of course, they made mistakes, but fortunately mostly not of a serious nature. But one, tending a switch, threw it before the rear truck of the *Nomad* had crossed, resulting in the rear truck taking a different track than the forward truck. The car rolled heavily and overturned, with considerable damage and one personal injury, a broken leg.

The business cars were the heaviest passenger equipment on the narrow gauge lines, weighing several tons more than other cars, and had a tendency to roll more heavily on poor or not-well-maintained track.

Experienced Passenger

During a trip when the line was being reballasted, but long sections not yet fully aligned, the *Nomad* noticeably, even alarmingly, rolled from side to side. A passenger was former Detroit, Toledo & Ironton President Charles Towle, who became so alarmed that he took a seat in the middle of the car—and urged me to do the same.

At Silverton this very experienced railroader examined the trucks of the car, calling attention to the depressed and obviously too weak springs. This contributed to the eventual rolling over of the car when the switch was prematurely thrown.

A major problem on the Silverton, especially during the dry season, was fires. A small weed or brush fire started by locomotive sparks (steep canyon walls along the right-of-way did not help), could quickly grow into a large fire, creating its own strong drafts.

The D&RGW "cinder bonnet" was not as effective as desired. It was made of a heavy mesh that extended some six inches or more above the top of the stack, being held secure by screw bolts on the side of the stack. Under the steady climb of the Silverton, the mesh would burn out, allowing sparks to be emitted. I suggested to the railroad that perhaps the very successful Colorado & Southern Ry. cinder catching device might be the answer. I obtained a scale drawing of this "bear trap" design from John Maxwell and gave it to the Durango & Silverton.

One was made for a K-36 Class engine and was tried out; it was an instant success. Familiar enough to railfans from pictures of the C&S trains on the South Park Line, it was a strange addition to the D&S. It not only reduced the number of escaping sparks, but gathered the cinders in a long pipe that extended down to the pilot truck; at water stops, the fireman could "drain" it and douse the hot sparks.

One of the major cosmetic improvements that Bradshaw instigated was the removal of the dummy diamond stacks from the three Class K-28 engines. Poorly-designed when first added in the 1950s, they were long scorned as the "goofy" stacks.

Equipment Back in Use

It was a pleasure to see former Rio Grande Southern 2-8-0 #42 return in the 1970s to Durango. I purchased it in 1953 from the dismantler of the RGS just to keep it from being scrapped. The dismantler was through, otherwise, with the task, and lacking an experienced crew to cut up the engine, then sitting at Durango, he collared me one day and said, "I have a proposition you can't refuse." In short, he told me he would sell me the engine for $1,200, and as I told him I had spent all I could on buying RGS relics, he went on to say I could pay for it at the rate of $100 a month. Ed and Paula Landrum of Dallas urged me to buy the locomotive, and loaned me the $2,000 it was going to cost by the time I got it on my property at South Alamosa.

Then the new Magic Mountain park near Denver wanted a narrow gauge engine, and I agreed to sell the #42. Magic Mountain had the engine refueled and converted to an oil burner, and it ran briefly before the park crashed into bankruptcy.

Eventually #42 was sold to the D&S, who planned to restore it for specials, movies, etc. The 1887 boiler checked out fine. The engine had been D&RG #420 until it was sold to the RGS in 1916.

It was also great to see former D&RGW caboose #0500 nicely rebuilt with a bright red coat of paint, and made available commencing in 1998 for groups to charter on Silverton trips.

In 1949 I'd seen the car arrive at Alamosa, obviously long out of use, and learned it had been recommended the car be scrapped. For the net salvage value of $125, the car was ours. It served for many years as a symbol of advertising for the motel and something for guests to happily inspect. Then for a while in the 1970s it served at Cripple Creek as the Chamber of Commerce office, lettered for the Florence & Cripple Creek R.R.

As the F&CC had ex-D&RG cabooses like the #0500, the lettering, I thought, was not really inappropriate. Prices of narrow gauge cabooses had meanwhile evidently mirrored the demand, and the virtual non-existent supply, and the #0500 changed hands for around $10,000!

New New Name for an Old Line

I had a hand in selection of the name for the Durango & Silverton. Right after Bradshaw purchased the line, I was at lunch with the new railroad owner and Alexis McKinney, who was helping him with negotiations and planning. The subject of the name of the new company came up. I urged a typical railroad name for its advertising appeal, and emphasized the southwestern area and character of the railroad, so we agreed that Durango & Silverton Narrow Gauge Railroad would be the name.

Engine #375, previously numbered #431, a 2-8-0, readies at Durango in 1945 with a stock train destined for Silverton. The locomotive, built in 1916, was from the Crystal River Railroad. It was dismantled in Pueblo in 1949. *Robert W. Richardson, collection of Mallory Hope Ferrell*

D&RGW #375 with the stock train shown on the previous page in Silverton in 1945. *Robert W. Richardson, collection of Mallory Hope Ferrell*

I had always been impressed with the importance of the name, ever since I encountered the Midland Terminal Ry. when it was abandoned. The name made it appear to be a switching road, the type of carrier most rail buffs and historians ignore. But the MT was an over-the-road line with interesting history and equipment, even a successor in part to the famed Colorado Midland. But the word "Terminal" in the name relegated the MT to the shadows. Thus, choosing the right name helps endear people to a particular railroad.

This is a typical Silverton train during the 1950s. Mudhen #463 was used to substitute for the #473 (which had the Grande Gold paint job). The trains still carried a caboose for the crew because it was a mixed train by the timetable. The glass-roofed *Silver Vista* is the rear car and was to be seen on most trips until it was destroyed in an Alamosa shop fire. At Hermosa, the grade increases considerably and the engine is working hard, as the 10-car consist was heavy.

OPPOSITE. A double-headed freight train on September 16, 1948 heads through Rockwood on its way to Silverton. *Robert W. Richardson, collection of Mallory Hope Ferrell*

Engine #495 switches at Aztec, New Mexico on the Farmington Branch line. Pipe trains were often seen in the 1950s and 1960s.

Three

FARMINGTON & THE LAND OF THE NAVAJO

he Farmington and Silverton branches had much in common. Both were about the same mileage, both followed the Animas River, but just as they went in opposite directions from Durango, so they were opposites in other ways.

The Silverton ambled amidst towering mountains along a rushing river. The Farmington Branch had an easier grade following a subdued Animas, amid typical dusty northern New Mexico landscape. There wasn't any High Line, so passengers could look down some 300 feet.

Railfans used up all their film on the Silverton, but spared very little for the Farmington. The branch just couldn't compete in attraction with the railroad trackage departing Durango in three other directions. So it was with me. I ventured out seldom with the camera to Bondad, Aztec and Farmington. I just didn't feel the branch was worth the attention after getting up at dawn on a day off to drive from Alamosa with hopes of catching some action in the San Juan Basin.

The branch had two traffic booms, a large amount of oil shipped in the '20s which then tapered off in the '40s. Then the pipe boom of the '50s strained the meager sid-ings and yard trackage at Farmington. A reluctant management forced to handle the traffic, extended some sidings, but switching on the branch still was a problem, emphasized one day by a weary conductor phoning Durango to inform them his engine was hopelessly "sewed up" and couldn't get free to return to Durango, and to send another engine to get them out of the mess. It was quite a change from earlier times when a few loads of apples might be a large ship-ment to handle.

The branch ended its days with the Farmington yard full of box cars, somehow forgotten or overlooked. The pipe people had been using them, literally, as storage for incoming fittings and drilling muds, and after the track was gone, the company sold the cars as is and where is, at a bargain price for the lot.

What Did They Haul?

In the final decades of the D&RGW narrow gauge, the type of traffic indicated a precarious future. There wasn't anything that supplied a heavy volume to the freight trains. So it was a little of this and a little of that, with the largest shippers going out of business or ship-ping over the highways.

Metal mining had been the lure of constructing much of the narrow gauge mileage, but by the 1950s it was almost entirely gone, even on the standard gauge lines. Of course the optimists predicted a great tonnage from one ore or another but usually nothing materialized. Even coal had deserted the railroad lines. Lumber had declined to just occasional carloads, with the vast forests of Ponderosa gone.

Westbound freight from Alamosa, except for the pipe boom traffic for a few years in the '50s, was simply a mixture of cars of one thing or another, like occasionally a car or two of autos or machinery for Dolores, before the main roads were paved.

Tank cars of oil would come to Alamosa from Chama, and a few loads of lumber from the irregularly-operated sawmills. From Monero and Durango came coal for the Alamosa power plant until it changed to natural gas. Some lumber came from Durango. Other points on the line shipped very little of anything, and most sidings were not used.

Until early in 1953 concentrates were shipped from Silverton and then the last mine closed. The market for lead and zinc was poor, and net sales didn't pay the cost of mining.

From the RGS came many cars of pinto beans originating from Dolores and Mancos. The last big sawmill at McPhee burned and was never rebuilt. Cars of box shooks came from Mancos until the match company

closed. Mines at Rico and Telluride, the principal shippers, went to trucks in 1951, giving up on irregular service and what they considered high rates.

The Ouray Branch occasionally had a car or two of ore; a train every two or four weeks sufficed. The rest of the branch and the remnant of the old main line toward Cerro Summit provided some shipments of seasonal produce and, in the fall, sugar beets.

With closing of the last coal mine at Crested Butte, about 90% of the traffic from the Gunnison lines vanished. There were a few cars now and then of Baldwin coal, but after the Black Canyon and Valley Line abandonments, this traffic went to trucks. Sapinero provided lumber shipments but not enough to keep alive all those miles of line.

Every year there was a variable amount of sheep and cattle that went to market, but abandonments, paving of roads and the D&RGW's reluctance to handle traffic it didn't want to be bothered with, and was convinced was profitless, was their doom.

In short, what freight traffic was left was not enough to share with trucks and good roads. That the Narrow Gauge lasted as long as it did was in large part due to the slowness of the coming of good roads—hard surface roads in Colorado—and determined highway operations to keep those roads open year around. And management's firm purpose was to

ABOVE. Sometimes during the Farmington pipe rush cars were left on the main track for unloading as siding tracks were scarce. The crews often had a difficult time finding a space for all the pipe cars.

OPPOSITE LEFT. Engine #495 with a long pipe train drifts down the Farmington Branch shortly after picking up its train at Carbon Junction. The distant San Juans have a heavy cover of snow.

The Farmington Branch

Carbon Jct.
Durango
Grubbs
Posta
Sunnyside
Bondad
Colmex
Hendrix
Cedar Hill
Perry
Inca
Aztec
Flora Vista
Hood
FARMINGTON

R. v.

rid itself of branch lines, all narrow gauge and all passenger trains. It even developed Rio Grande Motorways to siphon off the freight, passenger and mail business from its own rail lines. This accomplished, Motorways was itself discontinued.

Silver Toned Bells and Rails

As locomotives became older, they acquired a sort of individuality. One oldtimer stopped by one day and commented on the tone of #346's bell, which he claimed was due to silver in the metal mix when it was cast. He thought it had been done way back in 1881, when the D&RG supposedly supplied Baldwin Locomotive Works with silver for that purpose.

To illustrate his point that silver had given a special character to the bell, he picked up an angle bar and steel spike, and standing beside the engine, tapped the two pieces together and from the bell came a faint "ding."

He then stood beside another engine and tapped the two pieces, but there wasn't any acknowledging ring from that bell. Was it really because one bell had a bit of silver in its composition and the other had none?

Did Baldwin in 1881 regularly add a little silver to their bells? Perhaps some bell fancier can answer that.

Ranchers, and others wanting a dinner call, would hang a short piece of rail, where it could be hit with a hammer or similar tool, to make a

FARMINGTON BRANCH
Narrow Gauge

BRIEF DESCRIPTION OF LINE FROM PHYSICAL AND CONSTRUCTION STANDPOINT

Built Carbon Junction to Farmington as Standard Gauge in 1905 but changed to Narrow Gauge in 1923. Length is 47.68 miles with about 18 miles in Colorado and remainder in New Mexico. Line is in fairly open country and follows the Las Animas River throughout with moderate grade and alignment. Maximum grade is 1 per cent and maximum curve is 7 degrees.

Line is laid with about 13 miles of 65 pound rail and 34 miles of 75 pound, all of which was put in at time of construction - 1905.

Line is without special ballast other than native earth.

ESTIMATED INVESTMENT COST TO DECEMBER 31, 1947

Val. Sec. Colo. 17-D 451,116.81
" " N.M. 3 595,317.71 1,046,434.52

NORMAL MAINTENANCE ORGANIZATION

Section -2 foremen with gangs of 1 man in Winter, up to 3 men in Summer for each section.
B&B -1 gang with foreman and 6 men covers territory Chama to Durango and Silverton and Farmington branches.
Water Service -1 pipefitter covers territory Chama to Durango and Silverton and Farmington branches.

D & R G W Form 3250
Sec. 8
D & S L Form 1196

ALAMOSA FEB 28 ---- 19 51 ---

TRAIN ORDER NO 4 ---

To C&E ENG 484 ---- Opr. ---- M.

At CHAMA ---- X ----

ENG 493 RUN EXTRA FARMINGTON TO DURANGO AND HAS RIGHT OVER EXTRA 496 EAST CARBON JCT TO DURANGO AND WAIT AT CARBON JCT UNTIL TWO FIFTEEN 215PM FOR EXTRA 496 EAST ENG 496 RUN EXTRA DURANGO TO GATO AND HAS RIGHT OVER EXTRA 484 WEST DURANGO TO GATO AND HELP EXTRA 484 WEST GATO TO DURANGO
ENG 484 RUN EXTRA CHAMA TO DURANGO

RSE
Chief Dispatcher

CONDUCTOR, ENGINEMAN AND REAR TRAINMAN MUST EACH HAVE A COPY OF THIS ORDER

Made Con Time 1121 A M. Mosche Opr.

Train order for movements off the Farmington Branch and for Helper to go from Durango to Gato to assist westbound train.

Commodities Handled On The Farmington Branch
Years 1941 and 1948

Commodities	1941 Cars	1941 Tons	1941 System Revenue	1948 Cars	1948 Tons	1948 System Revenue
Local Freight Originated At And Destined to Points On The Branch						
Gasoline	173	3,797	$ 1,680	37	784	$ 1,101
All LCL Freight		1	67			17
	173	3,798	$ 1,747	37	784	$ 1,118
Freight Moved From Branch Points To System Points And To Branch Points from System Points						
Flour, Wheat	2	24	$ 54			$
Flour, Edible, NOS	2	23	140			
Mill Products, NOS	2	28	217			
Apples, Fresh, Not Frozen	1	15	137			
Potatoes, Other than Sweet				13	162	2,610
Beans & Peas, Dried	4	151	1,305	1	48	516
Horses, Mules, Ponies & Asses				1	8	36
Cattle & Calves, SD	28	256	996	33	324	1,773
Sheep & Goats, SD	8	48	240			
Sheep & Goats	128	1,031	2,836	18	180	484
Bituminous Coal				12	518	1,189
Salt	6	120	745			
Posts, Poles & Piling, NOS				6	71	670
Lumber, Shingles & Lath				18	228	1,235
Gasoline	417	9,169	19,839	29	616	2,521
Fuel, Road & Pet. Res. Oils, NOS	139	3,398	10,721	70	1,680	7,197
Fertilizers, NOS				8	105	1,142
Cast Iron Pipe & Ftgs, NOS				9	139	2,199
Iron & Steel Pipe & Ftgs, NOS				1	8	221
Automobiles, Passenger	2	6	177			
Ammunition & Explosives				12	70	2,059
Cement: Natural & Portland	44	989	6,715	165	3,742	33,861
Brick NOS & Building Tile	4	64	549			
Artificial Stone, NOS	1	30	267			
Lime, NOS	1	20	164			
Plaster: Stucco & Wall				4	60	654
Sewer Pipe & Drain Tile (Not Metal)	27	139	1,258			
Wallboard				1	8	45
Sugar	16	242	2,471			
Food Prods NOS, Not Frozen	10	171	1,193	5	46	683
Soap & Washing Compounds				3	19	112
Feed, Animal & Poultry, NOS				16	212	2,140
Manufactures & Miscel.	25	335	2,346	1	10	25
All LCL Freight		1,103	22,275		445	12,958
Total	877	17,362	$74,645	426	8,699	$74,330

A water car was often carried on Farmington Branch trains, as water supplies were meager and section crews had to be supplied. The Farmington tank was the newest on the system, replacing a tank that had burned.

resounding clang to announce it was meal time. Or to sound an alarm. A railroader told how the ranchers would ask for a piece of rail with markings of the Colorado Coal & Iron Co. which had started rail production in 1882. The ore used came from the Orient Mine, located on the eastern side of the San Luis Valley a few miles from Poncha Pass. The D&RG had built a line in 1881 over Poncha Pass from Mears Junction to reach the Orient Mine, which provided plenty of traffic for the next 40 years. The ore contained a fair amount of silver. The railroader showed how well the CC&I rail "rang" when a piece was suspended, and then from a few feet away he tapped two spikes together, the metal giving out a clear sound from the rail. Then he did this with another piece of rail that came from back East, and there wasn't any response in sound from the rail.

Narrow Gauge Track Material

Often someone refers to a "narrow gauge spike" or a piece of "narrow gauge rail," but in fact, there really isn't any such track item. The rails, spikes, splice bars, angle bars and switchstands were used alike on both gauges.

The D&RG's builders figured that with the small light cars and locomotives they could employ 30-pound rail (30 pounds to the yard) for their lines, saving a great deal in the cost of construction. At the time rail was rolled in lighter weights for use in mine tracks and industry generally, but 30-pound was considered just right for track for railroad pur-

poses. At the time, in the early 1870s, many standard gauge lines used rail of that weight and few got much above 56# in weight.

So the first steel rails rolled at Pueblo's Colorado Coal & Iron Co. in 1882 was 30# for the newly building Silverton extension from Durango. It was good rail, and a lot of it could be found in yards or sidings to the end. Because of the dry Colorado climate, the markings can still be clearly seen.

Heavy traffic, especially on the steeper grades, soon showed a need for heavier rail and much 35-, 40-, 45-pound rail was used as replacement rail and on the newer branches. Rail of 30# was three inches high, and 45# was about $4^{1}/_{4}$ inches high. All classes of D&RG 2-8-0s could operate over the lighter weights, but it was found that 45# was best when the new 2-8-2 Mudhens arrived. They simply broke any 30# rail they ventured upon.

As the D&RG standard gauged its main lines, the narrow gauge received the discarded rail and so eventually most of the narrow gauge had 70# rail by the 1920s. By the end, 85- or even 90-pound rail could be found in some stretches.

Spikes, too, evolved in size with an increase in the size of rails. Standard spikes of the time, about four inches in length, were enough in the 1870s, and most of the early spikes were cast iron, which became brittle and were not suited for re-use. As rails got larger, so did spike sizes, and

Caboose #0540 was built in 1923 to replace a car of that number destroyed in a wreck. It is still in use on the Durango & Silverton Narrow Gauge RR. Prior to the 1960s, passengers on the Silverton Mixed often rode in the caboose, especially when the combination baggage-coach was crowded. In earlier years the crew invited railfan passengers to ride the top of the cupola to better enjoy the scenery and take photos. Bob Richardson rode on the cupola on his first trip in 1941. *Henry Bender*

Caboose #0573 was built in 1885 in the first group of eight-wheel cabooses; it was just 17 feet long. It was given automatic couplers and automatic air brakes in 1903. The caboose was donated to Pioneer Park in Utah and is now on display at the Ogden, Utah Railroad Museum.

OPPOSITE LEFT. Engine #495 and a water car is seen at Farmington in the 1960s. The water car was used to fill section house cisterns on the branch.

there are many kinds of spikes including some unusual patented ones, like the triangular-bodied ones used in the 1870s on original lines in the Royal Gorge area.

Both the D&RG and RGS bought large quantities of an 1888 patent spike with a double head, one above the other, with a tapered flat wedge-shaped body. These were good for holding rails up to about 60#, but thereafter lost the advantages claimed. Sectionmen disliked them, so they aren't rare today, thanks to them being tossed along the right-of-way.

To connect the smaller rails of 35# or less, a simple splice bar was used, a flat piece of metal drilled with four holes. Its weakness was to break at the joint. Angle bars for 40# and heavier rail were used; they had more metal in a flange that rested on the base of the rail and were much stronger and not so likely to crack at the rail joint.

The patent office was inundated with all kinds of track inventions, and a few actually were put to use. Some were odd indeed. The South Park adopted the Fisher Rail Joint, which instead of being applied to the sides of the joining rails, was plate spiked to the ties, on which the rails rested and were held firmly by the clamps of inverted U-bolts. They did a good job and lasted until the tracks were torn up. Some were still in use in a smelter yard in Denver into the 1960s.

Until the 1880s the stub switch was used everywhere. The harp stand without a lamp was used. Split switches took over on main lines everywhere, but stub switches held out on yard and branch trackage until heavier engines ruled them out. Alamosa yard was all stub switches until about 1925. Accidents at night forced installation of switchstands with lamps, and the old harp stands were discarded or employed only in yards or for derails. Stub switches required constant checking to keep them functioning properly, meaning mainly that the rails would meet properly.

In the beginning tieplates weren't used, but soon the need was apparent to keep ties in good shape. The first ones were just metal stampings which cracked and broke when heavier engines were used. Gradually they were made heavier to withstand the use. But on much of the narrow gauge lines tieplates were not used.

Another track item that puzzles many who find them along abandoned grades are rail braces. These were employed to hold rails in line on curves. The first ones on the D&RG were a simple piece of iron or steel, with a couple of spike holes with the metal bent to fit up under the lip of the rail. These expanded to many styles; some were castings, others heavy steel and, of course, varied in size with the size of the rails. Some looked like a knuckle to fit against the rail, bracing the head of it.

Engine #346 and RGS caboose #0404 sit at the Colorado Railroad Museum in 1963. The triangle herald was designed for our own railroad named the Golden City & San Juan Railroad.

Engine #346 and RGS Caboose #0404 operating at the Colorado Railroad Museum in 1963.

Another puzzling prize for the hiker of abandoned grades is the "compromise block." This was a rectangular casting whose purpose was to equalize the meeting of two different weights of rails. They often had markings to indicate the weights of rails they were intended to fit under, and in addition could be found a nice "D&RG" in raised letters.

A number of combinations are found like 30 and 40, 30 and 45, 30 and 52, and 35 and 45. Being castings (produced at the D&RG's big foundry), naturally they broke, and the broken pieces puzzle many. Later, compromise pieces were of steel and were much heavier and often compromise angle bars are found for various combinations for rails.

The rails themselves bear evidence of many manufacturers. They came from mainly Eastern plants, but some came from England, especially rails bearing dates in the 1870s. Barrow Steel supplied a lot of rail. I never found any Krupp markings except on mine rail of 20# or lighter, some of it being used to strengthen the housing of the covered turntable of the Silverton Railroad. The 30# steel rail used on La Veta Pass in 1877 came from the steel mill at Johnstown, Pennsylvania. Iron rail with early dates could be found along the South Park, and some rails to support telegraph lines were old iron rails from the original 1869 trackage of the Union Pacific.

Rail on the Narrow Gauge had remarkably long life, and at times torn up rail was in good condition, suitable for relay. This is largely accounted for by the relatively light weight of engines and cars compared with standard gauge which are heavier and carry heavier loads. Rail of 40# laid on the south end of the RGS in 1891 was still in good condition

D&RGW rails bear evidence of many manufacturers. This picture shows a stub switch.

Kind of equipment Locomotive			No. 497						Class K-37	
Date	A.F.E.	Description of Work		Orig. Cost		Book Value		Depreciation		
								Began	Amount	
9-30	4569	D. & R.G.W.		22,575	52	22,575	52	10-1-30		
	4569	Credit				48	32	9-1-31		
	T-6302	Brakeman's cabin				124	04	8-1-37		
	T-7268	Priest flanger				191	75	9-1-39		
	T-7537	Mul. wear steel wheels				222	78	3-1-40		
	T-8705	Cyclone front end				412	20	9-1-41		
	T-8628	Cab Heater				41	72	12-1-41		
	T-9242	Schlooks Lubricator				267	51	12-1-42		
	GMA 303	Pilot plow (Charged to expenses) Applied Dec. 1944								

Retired			File No.		Changed From 1003	To 497	Date Sept. 1930	
When		Why	Where					
Book Value								
Individual's & Co's Bill					Remarks: **First trip, Sept. 6, 1930**			
Salvage								
Accrued Depreciation								

Kind of equipment Locomotive			No. 481					Class K-36 -189	
				Orig. Cost		Book Value		Depreciation	
Date	A.F.E.	Description of Work						Began	Amount
9-25	2406	Baldwin Loco. Works		27,898	04	27,898	04	10-1-25	
	2406			52	62	52	62	11-1-25	
	2660	Brick Arch and Tunes				68	71	7-1-26	
	3950	Cab curtains				33	92	1-1-29	
	5183	Brakeman's cupola				121	78	7-1-34	
	T-8021	Priest flanger				161	69	7-1-40	
	T-8019	Cab Heaters				43	45	1-1-41	
	T-9150	Cyclone front ends				412	74	7-1-42	

Retired				File No.		Changed From	To	Date
When		Why		Where				
Book Value								
Individual's & Co's Bill						Remarks: Ownership plates removed Oct. 1928		
Salvage						Automatic Fire door.		
Accrued Depreciation								

Kind of equipment Locomotive			No. 478					Class 148 - K-28	
				Orig. Cost		Book Value		Depreciation	
Date	A.F.E.	Description of Work						Began	
10-23	887	American Locomotive Company		34,270	34	34,270	34	11-1-23	
12-23	780	Trust plates		2	50	2	50	1-1-24	
12-23	887	Additional charges		52	03	52	03	1-1-24	
12-23	887	Credit Dec. allowance		60	15	60	15	1-1-24	
11-23		American Locomotive Works		34,270	34	33,348	69	1-1-25	
	2660	Brick arch and tubes				75	49	7-1-26	
	3950	Cab curtain; storm windows				41	69	1-1-29	
	T-6077	Air Sig. & Stm. heat appliances				239	78	8-1-37	
	T-8020	Brakeman's Cabin				135	65	1-1-41	
	T-8326	Automatic Air Brakes				22	71	1-1-41	
	T-8019	Cab Heaters				43	45	1-1-41	
	T-8655	Multiple wear tender wheels				216	90	1-1-42	
	T-9634	Pilot Plow				540	25	12-1-42	
						34,664	61		

Retired				File No.		Changed From	To	Date
When		Why		Where				
Book Value								
Individual's & Co's Bill						Remarks: Spark deflector applied Ala. Oct. 1937.		
Salvage						Automatic Fire door.		
Accrued Depreciation								

Charts courtesy Colorado Railroad Museum Archives and Tom Fitzgerald

60 years later. West of Antonito 70# rail laid as secondhand in the early 1920s was still in good condition at the time of abandonment. When the RGS dismantled, pieces of rail dating to the very earliest of the D&RG system, 1870, were found. Other dates in the 1870s were found on logging grades, indicating their purchase was secondhand from the D&RG.

The Union Pacific had so much iron rail of the 1860s removed from its original line by the 1890s that Colorado roadmasters were required to use it in yards and spurs despite their protests. Management decreed it must be so employed, although much of it, like most old iron rail, was deemed to be scrap.

The last trackage that included original iron rail was the Baldwin Branch. Into the 1930s this trackage still had the original iron rail laid in 1882, and an inspection reported the track unsafe at any speed. The iron had crystallized and would break. The Colorado & Southern got rid of this line in the 1930s by giving it to the D&RGW and also supplying heavier relay rail just removed from its old main line to Pueblo.

Much of the South Park had 40# rail, a good amount of it laid by the Colorado & Southern in the early 1900s. Such is the rail to be found at Alpine Tunnel, for instance.

Water Not Drinkable

It was a couple of years after moving to Colorado that I realized that drinking the water in most of the mountain areas was not a prudent thing to do, and for most of the time I lived in Colorado, I simply avoided drinking the water anywhere except in several cities.

After I had been sick a couple of times, and both times it was definitely attributed to unsafe water, I learned from a party of state health department people who were briefly staying at the motel, that I had assumed wrongly that the water in the mountains was safe. Far from it. I am glad to say 50 years later that great improvements have been made.

Back then if one asked a waitress about the water, there was always the prompt assurance that it came from the mountains (in the middle of them, where else could it come from?) and was pure.

At Silverton the supply was a gulch running with clear sparkling cold water. It was fresh water from snowbanks higher up, the gulch flow being diverted somewhat to the city mains with the entrance having a sort of steel grating which kept out tree branches, rocks, and anything else that could be measured from entering the mains. That was Silverton's filtering system in total!

A young friend went to work with crews that were standard gauging the Monarch Branch. It was thirsty work, and he was assured by his elders that he should just go ahead and drink the water flowing down the streams from the mountains, assuring him it was about the purest one could find. After two weeks in the railroad hospital at Salida, he went home to St. Louis to recuperate.

It was a warm day, and I was snapping the final stock trains in September of 1951 on the Rio Grande Southern. I stopped for lunch at the cafe in Placerville and saw the waitress set glasses of ice tea before us. I reminded her that I hadn't ordered iced tea, but coffee. Her reply was that it wasn't ice tea at all, that was water, and they'd had some very windy days, and dust had blown into the water supply, accounting for the color of the water, making it appear to be iced tea! A little detour and we saw the water coming into town in an open ditch. We also discovered evidence that sheep or some type of wildlife had waded through that water.

I just assumed Durango's water was safe, but how wrong I was. In the spring of 1953 I was getting the #42 ready to be moved dead to Alamosa; it was warm work on a warm day. I made a number of trips to the water cooler in the roundhouse. We had to remove the engine's main rod, then bush the driver pins and make sure other parts wouldn't move or get lost during the trip. Late in the afternoon, the job completed, I drove to Ouray, and spent the night there at the old hotel that had an indoor swimming pool fed by the natural hot springs of the area.

The next morning I awoke late but had a strange lethargy; I just could not get up. It was as if something had paralyzed me, and with great effort and frequent stops to rest, I managed to get dressed in the next half hour. Feebly I made it down the stairs and told the lady manager how I felt, and she recommended I go up to Dr. Spangler's, the town physician who also ran the hospital. I had to make myself get in the car and drive up there.

There were a number of people seated in the waiting room, and I joined them. I must have passed out, as the next thing I knew I awoke with people talking around me, one of them obviously the doctor, who was asking what happened and they told him, "He just sort of slid onto the floor, doc." Even to open my eyes was an effort, but finally I made it into his examination room, where he quizzed me as to where I had been.

When I told him of drinking all that ice water in Durango he indicated he knew the problem, commented briefly that it was unsafe and that people should be warned, that the authorities were aware of the problem, but they just hushed it up.

I forgot what he gave me for my illness, but he advised that I get home to Alamosa and just rest and take the medicine prescribed. He warned me strongly that when driving, if I felt drowsy or inattentive, to not wait until the next town, but immediately to pull off the road and just shut my eyes and rest, and not to resume driving until I was fully awake.

With that advice, I took off for what was my slowest trip back. It was 35 miles to Montrose, then 56 mostly rough gravel road miles to Gunnison, 65 miles over Monarch Pass to Poncha Springs, 26 more over Poncha Pass to Mineral Hot Springs, then 53 straight, monotonously flat gravelly miles to Alamosa. Oh what a long trip it was, with occasional naps and stops for a soft drink or hot tea.

It was about two weeks before I got back my normal feeling, and I could move about without making myself do it.

I could go on and cite numerous examples of people becoming sick by bad water. Like the Gunnison "goop" they laughed about, caused by a poorly engineered water system being invaded now and then by the waters of the Slate River, which in turn drained the Crested Butte area.

Or the family of Texans with a very sick and feverish teenager, having cut short their summer vacation in the Creede area. They told of staying at a camp and plying the lad with plenty of water, thinking that would improve him! The health people said they had tried unsuccessfully to close the place down because of the unsafe water. No wonder the kid got even sicker the longer he remained in the camp.

The health people were stymied in getting legislation through Colorado's assembly to remedy matters. The rural members blocked any attempt to regulate water, let alone force any community to admit the state of affairs.

At one point the health department wanted to do what some other states had done—simply place a sign at the city limits to the effect that the water supply was "approved," or something to that effect. This, they thought, might force the stubbornest places to improve things.

One time a couple of new salesmen to the area stopped overnight at the motel, one feeling bad and having the symptoms of having consumed either bad food or water. He was very thirsty, and I told him to drink all he wanted at Alamosa, but not anywhere else, and when I learned their next stop was Durango, I told him he'd have to exist on carbonated drinks, hot tea or coffee, and to certainly not drink any Durango water.

While at Durango he declined to drink any water, and when asked why, he told them what I'd said. Later I was severely criticized for telling them the facts. Durangoans didn't deny the water problems, but they were angry that anyone mentioned them! I stuck to my guns and had several hot arguments on the subject. They calmed down somewhat when I told them it was a matter that eventually was going to get in the press, and then they would have a lot of publicity they sure wouldn't enjoy.

Alamosa had safe water by accident. So did our motel. The water supply was from artesian wells, and the water was purified by a natural filtering system through great depths of sand from a rock formation 1,500 or more feet down.

When the Alamosa railroad shop was razed and most railroad operations removed, years afterward a huge artesian well that had supplied the railroad was still roaring away and apparently draining into the nearby Rio Grande River, as someone had forgotten the well which was not readily noticeable, hidden by a wooden cover in the abandoned roundhouse area. Twenty years after the Narrow Gauge was gone, this water was still being wasted.

Photographer Otto Perry

It was my good fortune to get to know Otto C. Perry at a time when he was still actively taking pictures. I even accompanied him on part of several of his trips.

Otto had been at it, he told me, since 1912, and one time he told of riding his bicycle from Denver to Colorado Springs to take pictures of Colorado Midland Railroad locomotives. Known best for his Colorado

In retirement, the #318 occasionally received a load of snow much as it had endured while in service on the D&RG and Florence & Cripple Creek.

Denver & Rio Grande Western Railroad Co.

SUMMARY

OF

EQUIPMENT

(Narrow Gauge)

January 1, 1948

KEY

SC .... Steel Center Sills.
SS .... Steel Super-structure.
WS ...... Wood Super-structure.
SUF ..... Steel Under Frame.
AC .... Air Conditioned.
FB .... Flat Bottom.
Dp ...... Dumps.
ET .... Engine Tender.
DD ..... Double Deck.

(Narrow Gauge) Freight

Series	Type			Count
32-78	Refgr.	40	Wood	37
150-169	Refgr.	50	Wood	20
3000-3749	Box	50	Wood	688
5500-5849	Stock	50	Wood	348
5900-5999	Stock	50	Wood	100
9029-9184	Coal	40	Wood	4
1000-1499	Coal	50	Wood	417
1500-1899	Coal	50	Wood	361
1900-1925	Coal	50	Wood	22
9200-9573	Coal	50	Wood	308
700-899	Coal Dp.	50	Wood	198
6200-6209	Flat	60	SCS	8
6210-6219	Flat	60	SCS	9
6300-6314	Flat	60	Wood	15
6500-6544	Flat	80	SUF	45
				2,578
04343-04982	Wood-Caboose			2
04990	Wood-Caboose			1
0500-0589	Wood-Caboose			21
				24

(Narrow Gauge) Passenger

Series	Type	Material	Count
54,60,122	Mail & Bagg.	Wood	3
65,66 & 119	Mail & Bagg.	Wood	3
111,127,163 to 169	Baggage	Wood	8
126	Baggage	Wood	1
212	Coach & Bagg.	Wood	1
310,312,323,325, 326,327	Coach	Wood	6
256,280,284,306, 319, 320	Coach	Wood	6
Alamosa	Parlor-Buffet	Wood	1
Durango & Chama	Parlor-Buffet	Wood	2
Silver Vista-313	Obsvn.	SS & Wood	1
Total Narrow Gauge Cars			32

NON-REVENUE EQUIPMENT (Narrow Gauge)

4	Business cars	B-1, B-2, B-3, B-7
5	M. & B. outfits	053, X-64, 0118, 0120, 0123
8	Coach outfits	0250-0252, 0270, 0274, 0291, 0292, 0307
2	Tourist outfits	0452, 0460
6	Water cars	0459 and 0465-0470
6	Water cars (E.T.)	W-488 to W-499
1	Excursion outfit	0566
86	Box outfits	04013-04999
13	Flat outfits....................	06008-06413 and 07407
2	Coal outfits	09160, 09163
1	Wedge snow plow	09271
1	Pile Driver	OB
11	Flangers	OC to OL and OT
3	Rotary snow plows	OM, OO and OY
1	Construction derrick	OP
6	Air dumps	OR, OS & 0140-0143
2	1 Jordan spreader	OU & 1 Spreader....OV
158		

MISCELLANEOUS EQUIPMENT

Gas-Electric Tractors	15
Gas-Electric Crane Cars	4
Gas-Electric Tractor Cranes	6
Gas-Electric Crane Trucks	7
Trucks	81
Maintenance of Way Motor Cars	389
Motor Inspection Cars	2
Bulldozer-Loader Tractors	16
Gasoline Draglines	16
Weed Burners	3
Rail Laying Machines	3
Station Wagons	5
Sedans	8
Carryall Scrapers	3
Coupes	2
Crawler Tractors	2
Reconnaissance Cars	2
Passenger Bus	1
Crawler Cranes	3

D&RGW NARROW GAUGE STEAM LOCOMOTIVES

January 1, 1948

SERIES	SERVICE	ROAD CLASS	TYPE	M.P. CLASS	TOTAL ENGINES	Diam. of Cyl	Stroke	Steam Press.	Diam. of Drivers	Weight on Drivers	Total Weight Including Loaded Tender	Tractive Power	Coal Cap. (tons)	Tender Water Capacity (gal.)	STOKERS			Super-Heater	Elesco F.W. Heater	EXHAUST STEAM INJECTORS				Year Built
															Duplex D-1	Simplex B	Standard Modified Type B			Elesco	Sellers	Syphon	Circulator	
268, 278	F	C-16	2-8-0	60 N.G.	2	15	20	160	36¾	59,335	122,110	16,540	6	2,500	......	......	......	......	......	......	......	......	......	1882
315-319	F	C-18		72 N.G.	4	16	20	145☐	38	64,000	129,000	16,606	7	2,300	......	......	......	......	......	......	......	......	......	1895-6
340, 345	F	C-19		70 N.G.	2	16	20	160	36¾	64,000	127,260	18,947	6	2,500	......	......	......	......	......	......	......	......	......	1881
360, 361	F	C-21		93 N.G.	2	17	20	160	38⅞	85,650	160,950	20,686	5	2,900	......	......	......	......	......	......	......	2.	......	1900
375	F	C-25		112 N.G.	1	18	20	170	38	107,400	181,400	24,641	6	3,000	......	......	......	......	......	......	......	1.	......	1903
452-464	F	K-27	2-8-2	125 N.G.	8	17	22	200	40	108,300	223,550	27,000	8.5	4,100	......	......	......	7.	......	......	......	......	......	1903
473-478	P	K-28		148 N.G.	3	18	22	200	44	113,500	254,500	27,540	8	5,000	......	......	......	3.	......	......	......	......	......	1923
480-489	F	K-36		189 N.G.	10	20	24	195	44	143,850	286,600	36,200	9.5	5,000	......	......	......	10.	......	......	......	......	......	1925
490-499	F	K-37		- N.G.	10	20	24	200	44	148,280	307,250	37,100	9	6,000	......	......	......	10.	......	......	......	......	1.	1928

☐ = 315

Engine #482, a Class K-36 built by Baldwin, started service in September of 1925. It could handle freight or passenger tonnage equally well. Engine #482 was retired in 1962 and delivered to the Cumbres & Toltec Scenic Railroad in 1970. *C.T. Felstead*

photos, actually Otto had traveled all over the U.S. using his camera to capture many rail scenes. His most common subject in Colorado was the Denver & Rio Grande Western Railroad, yet he had a strong dislike, one could even say "hatred," for the road's management, and he frequently expressed in strong terms what he thought of them.

The one incident that particularly got him in that frame of mind was at Grand Junction where railroad officials had called the police, and Otto was arrested and held in jail over the weekend. He was let go on Monday without charges, but the incident rankled him.

To shield the lens of his camera, Otto had the habit of using a telephone pole, and unlike most railfans, he usually had nothing to do with railroaders he encountered, seemingly avoiding them, seldom speaking to them. So enginemen and train crews, seeing this figure, as they thought, trying to conceal his presence behind a telegraph pole, viewed him with suspicion.

Several times I've had railroaders describe Otto, and ask me if I knew who he was. They never suspected he was only using the poles to shield his camera lens.

Otto lived in his old black Ford, and often his very elderly mother was along, saying nothing, barely noticeable in the back seat. But he told me she greatly enjoyed traveling. In the back of the car he carried all sorts of rations, and I got the impression he never patronized restaurants. He would rustle around and bring forth a bag of ancient cookies, or perhaps some old candy. At Cumbres one time he built a little fire, opened a can of soup, and we had lunch on a hillside near Los Pinos tank.

That first spring in Colorado in 1949 he came by and persuaded me to go along with him to St. Elmo. He'd been on a trip and was on his way home. He pointed out I could get a late afternoon Motorway bus to Alamosa from Poncha Springs.

Heading up Chalk Creek Road we paused at the Mt. Princeton Hotel, a great rambling wooden affair of a long-gone period, long idle, yet intact. Apparently it had not been a success. Then we continued past the Chalk Cliffs on the gravel road on the South Park grade. Finally we reached deserted St. Elmo, its main street consisting of closed businesses, except for one, the Stark Brothers store, which had also been the community post office.

With a smile Otto predicted I would enjoy meeting the Starks and seeing the interior of the store. It was a cluttered place, and the post office boxes were still apparently full of mail, a method of filing for the owners.

An elderly sister and her brother still lived in the house behind and adjoining. She came out, and we each bought a soft drink, even though

Otto C. Perry in a typical pose. This photo was snapped at the Georgetown Loop site where he and the unidentified man at the right were attending a dedication.

just sitting in the shade it was cool enough. I bought a Hershey bar, which when unwrapped, indicated extreme age. Otto winked at me and then made the comment that St. Elmo was certainly an interesting ghost town. The old lady immediately erupted, "This isn't a ghost town. We live here. We're not ghosts!" and trailed off into angry mutterings.

Another trip was to Osier and Toltec Tunnel. The county had graded the road about as far as Sublette, and beyond it was just a rough trail. We finally came opposite of a sort of ridge that extended toward Toltec Gorge and the tunnel that pierced the end of the ridge. The terrain was rough and rocky, and the top of the ridge heavily forested, yet Otto drove the Ford across this until the trees stopped him. Otto had been hoping to snap the afternoon *San Juan* as it approached the Gorge.

Still another trip to Cumbres was made too early in the year and before we reached La Manga Pass Summit, there were huge drifts of old snow. Undaunted, Otto produced shovels, and we got by one, only to find the way blocked for hundreds of feet further on by snow, a good two feet or more deep. Otto was for trying to go around through what looked like an open space until I reminded him that was a mess of big rocks hidden by the snow.

Returning from that jaunt, as we reached a recently graded section of the road, I saw a flash like small lightning down by the gear shift, and finally Otto looked at it, and he pulled over.

It turned out that somewhere we'd hit something that had pushed the battery carrier up against the floor in such a way that occasionally it bounced enough that the battery would short on the frame of the car. No problem for Otto. He used an aspen pole from a nearby fence, and a rock for leverage, and pried the carrier back down.

One summer day I went along with him to Cumbres. Otto had in mind getting down to the vicinity of the steel trestle at Cascade Creek about a mile west of Osier. There was a road of sorts for about a mile from a turnoff midway between the Los Pinos water tank and the pass. Then the road vanished into a vague trail, but the going was very slow, and finally we could go no further as there was an impassable little gulch, even for Otto. We waited for the oncoming eastbound freight and settled for pictures of it on the other side of the mountain high above. As Otto was heading on to Durango, and I had a motel to look after, he dropped me off at the Cumbres Pass station to catch the *San Juan*. The train had a large summer load, and I sat with a few others on boxes in the baggage car.

On the occasion of the last four-engine train over Marshall Pass in 1954, Otto and I were the only photographers present. After photographing the train leaving Sargent at the western foot of the pass, I drove around over Monarch Pass, then up to Mears Junction and on the gravel road to Shirley Curve, driving just beyond a girder bridge to get my car out of sight of any picture taking. Then I hiked a short distance up the grade to wait for the three Helpers and the train.

As I stood there, here came Otto's Ford up to the bridge, and after parking, up the grade he came. A large bush was between us, and I was

ABOVE AND RIGHT. For the movie *Three Young Texans* filmed on the Farmington Branch, the #453 was fitted with a dummy balloon stack and a box headlight. Attempts to make the engines look "old-timey" often resulted in weird appearances.

certainly not in his sight. For fun—don't ask why—I uttered a loud but low-toned "Hurr-rrr-ry Otto—last tt-tt-train coming!" He stopped, looked all around but didn't seem the least bit frightened, I was relieved to note. And then resolutely he resumed hiking up the track to select a spot. No "ghost" was going to intimidate him!

About that time could be heard the distinctive "thumpa-thumpa-thumpa" occasionally of the water brake on a Helper engine, and soon the first K-36 came round the bend. A few minutes later came the second K-36 and not far behind, the third. We both were busy taking pictures, watching as they rounded the sharp curve over the little creek and headed

for Mears Jct. Eventually the low roar of the train itself could be heard, and it made quite a scene filling the big curve with the final Powderhorn stock shipment by rail.

As soon as it passed, Otto ambled down the track and to his car and was gone before I had any opportunity to reveal my presence and especially to explain that he hadn't been hearing ghost voices. It bothered my conscience, and I never got up enough nerve to tell him about it later.

Otto never made enlargements of his pictures. We wanted to use some of his pictures in a *Colorado Railroad Annual*, and he agreed to let us have enlargements made, but he declined to let the negatives out of his possession. Over the years he had enough misfortunes that he just didn't trust anyone with them. So I arranged to set up the enlarger and the chemical pans in a restroom of the museum, and Otto came out and brought the negatives and watched the process. He was amazed at how easy it was to make enlargements, and decided then and there he would do the same, but to the best of my knowledge, he never did.

Around the World in 80 Days

Around the World in 80 Days was filmed in the San Juan area in October of 1955. There were no longer any of the smaller engines available because all had been scrapped from the Alamosa-Durango line. The Army diesel was on hand, and an ingenious scheme was hatched to employ it

and the display C-18 Class #315 2-8-0. A dummy baggage car was built around the diesel. The #315 was repainted as the *Jupiter* of Union Pacific fame, and a steam and smoke-producing device was placed inside the firebox.

The engine had a cracked cylinder and other problems and could not be steamed up. But being trailed by the "baggage car" and three passenger cars in the Grande Gold yellow paint scheme, the resulting train was very realistic, with smoke belching from the diamond stack and steam from the cylinders.

The disguised diesel, however, was not used to power the train on its runs to location spots on the main line, such as to Ignacio, whose train

For the movie *Three Young Texans*, Mudhen #453 was slightly altered with a fake stack and box headlight. Because it had been numbered "8" there was a delay as crews argued that the train orders should use its actual D&RGW number.

station was disguised as "Fort Kearney." One of the K-28 Class locomotives would haul the train to and from location, then that engine would be uncoupled and placed on the opposite end of the train when filming involved one end or the other of the four-car train behind the "60."

In dropping down around the High Line where the K-28 couldn't be at either end, trainmen with brake clubs were stationed on all the car platforms to apply handbrakes if necessary. All in all, it was a very successful deception, and even railfans were puzzled at the "60" supposedly steaming along.

At Ignacio, Joe E. Brown played the part of the station agent, and there he was required to come out with his Irish paddy walk and speak one sentence to the travelers. He'd just barely get that far when the director would say "cut!" Over and over the scene was played, halted at times for long delays when a fleecy cloud would obscure the sun. And then there was a break for lunch. It certainly demonstrated why it took so long to film some movie scenes. A railroad clerk and I had gone over to watch the filming, and we got so bored at this we eventually went home, after waiting in vain for more action, especially with all the extras standing around. And in the finished movie as seen by theater-goers, the Joe Brown scene was not even used!

Harp Switchstands

The "harp" style switchstands at the Colorado Railroad Museum came mostly from the Rio Grande Southern at the time the line was torn up in 1952–53. Several came from the Ouray Branch of the D&RGW in 1954. These were cast new probably in 1881-1882 for the most part when the D&RG was expanding with hundreds of miles of track. At the time, such stub switches and styles of switchstands were common in the U.S. where switch lights were not being used to any great extent.

When the D&RG began standard gauging (at first simply three-railing) its narrow gauge lines, they continued to rely on stub switches. The need for switch lights forced employment of various rotary-style switchstands to replace the harps. Some of these switchstands also were cast in the D&RG foundry at Burnham Shops in Denver.

Thus when Otto Mears embarked on construction of his RGS in early 1890, the D&RG had a lot of surplus track material and construction material from the former narrow gauge lines, and especially in connection with the new track being completed west of New Castle of what was termed the Rio Grande Junction Ry. to Grand Junction for joint use with the Colorado Midland.

The arrival of the new standard gauge engines caused replacement of rail ranging from 30-pound and up, and laying 65- and even 85- pound rails, the latter not suited to be used with either stub switches nor harp stands. It was said the vibrations of the rails as heavy locomotives crossed such switches would shatter the cast harp stands.

In 1914, Colorado regulations required switch lights on all tracks where a passenger train passed after daylight hours. This forced replacement of harp stands on the main tracks of the RGS. Thereafter the harp stands were used for derails of the stub single rail variety and in yards. The surplus stands were sold to lumber roads which branched from the RGS at several points.

The D&RG harps weigh 220 pounds and stand seven feet tall. They differ from the DSP&P and Union Pacific harps in some ways in the shape of the base casting; also, the targets on the South Park harps had a double diamond on the rod. These were literally targets, a favorite target for random shooting and reckless use of firearms in small towns. One in the center of Dolores was riddled with such holes. Some targets were actually shot off the rod.

In use, the targets were bent because of winter ice and snow; in summer when the slide rails expanded, the switch was thrown only with great difficulty, earning among other phrases the designation of "head bashers" in an age innocent of hard hats.

The Missing K-28, Gone to Alaska

For more than 50 years a trio of Class K-28 2-8-2s have plied the Silverton Branch and are likely the most photographed narrow gauge locomotives. And, of course, many ask where are the other numbers of the 10 of this class that were new from Alco in 1923? The simplest answer is "gone to war," and like many who went on to WWII, they, too, never returned.

It all started in an uproar in southwestern Colorado in the spring of 1942 when headlines announced the Army was going to take so many engines from the D&RGW's narrow gauge that the company was being forced to shut it down and abandon operations forever.

But after some highly placed people, including a local judge, went to Washington to seek to save their rail transportation, the full truth didn't meet the headlines. The railroad management had been caught in a huge fib. The truth was that the U.S. Army needed some engines for its takeover of the White Pass & Yukon Railway in Alaska, but it had not asked for or indeed needed all the D&RGW's engines. The truth was that the railroad was trying to get the Army to take more than it wanted, so the D&RGW could shut down its narrow gauge operations.

When hearings were held in 1950 on the discontinuance of the *San Juan*, the key to continuing the Alamosa–Durango line, the thick file of clippings and letters was placed with the city manager, along with other material to be used in opposing the discontinuance. As the hearing date approached, the file drawer was found to be empty. Police checked many leads to the burglary, but the fact that nothing else was missing from the office led to finger pointing at who was to benefit from its vanishing.

In the summer of 1942 the 10 locomotives were closely examined, and seven of the ones in best condition were run through the shop for various needs. That fall they were shipped by barge from Seattle, destined for Whitehorse. The Army was not prepared to do any major shopping for the WP&Y. Neither, as the D&RGW had implied, were all the rotaries requisitioned; instead only ON was sent north.

For cars, the Colorado & Southern had a quantity it no longer needed, including a number of box cars that had been held for ice shipments from the South Platte Canyon. So the D&RGW was not stripped of needed cars.

After the locomotives went to Alaska, the D&RGW was left with 31 Mikado-type engines, of which eight were the oldest, the K-27 Mudhens. These proved adequate for the large increase in wartime traffic, moving lead and zinc, coal and limestone from the mountains, the last two items primarily for the Pueblo steel plant.

When the Army found a need for more three-foot-gauge engines, they scoured the country, but the long Depression had wiped out virtually all remaining narrow gauge motive power in the U.S. The East Broad Top in Pennsylvania had none to spare because their coal business kept their six Mikados busy, but they did let their sole 2-6-2 #11 go off during the war to some secret destination.

Of its five Ten-wheelers, the East Tennessee & Western North Carolina supplied two for Alaska, the #10 and #14. They ended up as rip-rap at the pier area.

The Colorado & Southern supplied its last two 1890-vintage (though much rebuilt) 2-8-0s #69 and #70, in addition to many cars. From the locked-up enginehouses at Silverton were requisitioned the last three engines of Mears little lines, Silverton Northern's trio of 2-8-0s #3 and #4, and the outside-frame 2-8-0 #34.

The result was that Army personnel had to make do with a large variety of engines of very different abilities as to tractive power and being able to cope with the extremely low temperatures encountered in the Alaskan winters.

Instances of tenders freezing were not unknown, and maintenance of exposed piping and appurtenances was difficult. From reports, the military relied mostly on the WP&Y's own larger engines and the K-28, with the smaller engines gradually set aside.

At war's end the WP&Y had no need of all this additional power, and so it was returned to Seattle by barge, with the #472 being sent back in 1944, at first destined to the Northern Pacific shops to repair some heavy damage. The other six locomotives were also brought back and placed in storage in the area until sold for scrap in 1946.

The #472 seemed likely to escape that fate, as it had been hauled to the Ogden, Utah Supply Depot, but it too was sold for scrap in 1946. The D&RGW meantime had declined any interest in re-acquiring the seven engines.

The engines and rotary used for rip-rap are being retrieved somewhat in recent years with expectation of being a historical display on the WP&Y. At low water they could be seen lying on their sides.

Harp switchstands of the 1880s were saved during the scrapping of the Rio Grande Southern, which had a number of stub switches in yards as well as stub derailers in sidings. These switchstands came to the RGS secondhand when the D&RG's main line was standard gauged in 1890.

An eastbound freight near Carbon Junction on the Farmington Branch pulls a string of pipe cars in the mid-1950s. *Robert W. Richardson, collection of Mallory Hope Ferrell*

This is a 1950 excursion at Monarch. The train had left Salida in the morning and traveled over Poncha Pass to Villa Grove, then returned to Poncha Junction to make the trip to Monarch. The size of the train was limited by the 4% grades and the switchback on the Monarch Branch.

Four

THE THIRD DIVISION:
GUNNISON TO SALIDA & THE VALLEY LINE

It's been nearly 50 years since I rode the cleanup train over Marshall Pass, sitting atop the caboose cupola. Watching the long string of empty stock cars snake ahead, I thought of all those trains of the past 70 years and how busy this line had been. Traffic on the last few miles into Salida must have been the heaviest of the entire narrow gauge, what with the coal from the Butte mine, iron ore from the Orient mine and limestone from Monarch.

No wonder Salida had the largest concentration of narrow gauge power, two roundhouses and was a 100% railroad town. No wonder it was selected as the site of the company hospital, what with all those break-in-twos and runaways on those passes during link-and-pin times.

A fall, 1945 trip when I was perched atop the caboose through the Black Canyon and over Cerro Summit, was another venture not easily forgotten. Neither were those intimidating 2,000-foot-high walls of the aptly-named Black Canyon, quiet Cimarron with its padlocked eating house and everything else locked and deserted. With the two Crystal River "little Mudhens" at the head, and a Mudhen behind the caboose, it was easy to imagine the

dense traffic that trackage handled when this was a bottleneck of a two-state main line.

The Gunnison country has always had a fascination which lasted through the last of its days; even now C-16s are displayed properly at Gunnison and Cimarron. The variety of operations of the Third Division with its branches, and remnants of the South Park, weren't to be seen elsewhere. Perhaps as you read this book some of my feelings will rub off on you...and watch out...you'll be exploring where those grades wander, and you'll join the many who take the U.S. 50 by-way on that grade over Marshall Pass.

Film was still rationed during my 1946 travels (rationing of XX and SuperPan was still in effect). I kept picking up a couple rolls here and there, and when vacation time came, I was astounded to see I had some 90 rolls of 616 on hand. Has any other fan descended on Colorado with that quantity?

I was going to make up for 1945 and enjoy not having to be stingy as I headed for the Gunnison country and the RGS. But the best of plans go astray...it rained and rained and was dark and gloomy, so most of that film hoard went back to Texas unused...to be squandered on

ABOVE. This 1880 view of Salida was taken when the town and the railroad were very new. The rails had only reached here in May and were pushed on to Leadville by July. The line to Gunnison used the wooden truss bridge over the Arkansas River. The new tracks stand out, as apparently they were not completely ballasted.

RIGHT. This is a rear view of the *Silver Vista* at Gunnison just before the train made the last excursion run through the Black Canyon in 1949. The 15 miles beyond Sapinero was abandoned in May of 1949.

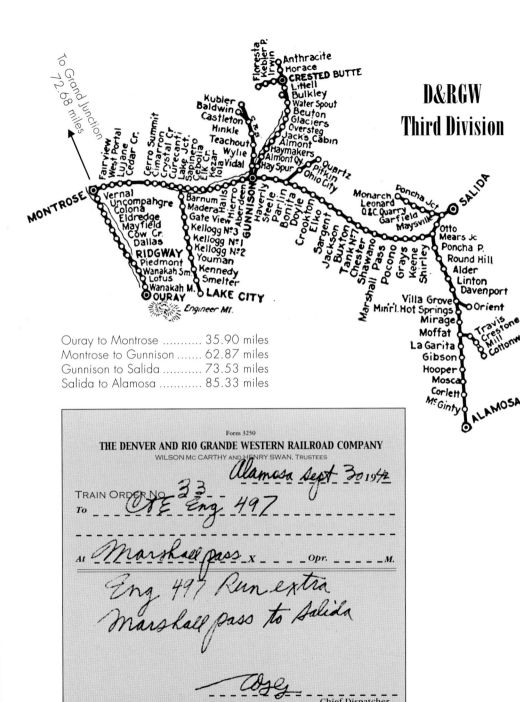

D&RGW Third Division

Ouray to Montrose .... 35.90 miles
Montrose to Gunnison .... 62.87 miles
Gunnison to Salida .... 73.53 miles
Salida to Alamosa .... 85.33 miles

Form 3250

THE DENVER AND RIO GRANDE WESTERN RAILROAD COMPANY
WILSON McCARTHY AND HENRY SWAN, Trustees

Alamosa Sept 30 1942

Train Order No. 33
To C&E Eng 497

At Marshall pass X Opr. M.

Eng. 497 Run extra
Marshall pass to Salida

Osey
Chief Dispatcher

CONDUCTOR, ENGINEMAN AND REAR TRAINMAN MUST EACH HAVE A COPY OF THIS ORDER

Made Com Time 702 P M. Baker Opr.

the Texas Electric and worn out steam, and I didn't have to buy another roll of film for the next six months.

To this day, whenever I think of the Gunnison lines I have to laugh at that unlucky September, all that film just having a roundtrip ride doing nothing useful. But it was still fun to watch a dripping #278 or #360 struggle with wet weeds, while a soaked fireman pounded clogged sand pipes. Those are some of my fond memories...I hope you enjoy them.

The Old Main Line to Gunnison

In 1948 and the next several years after, if you were to ask the Yard-master or Trainmaster at Salida when the next train might be operated west over Marshall Pass, you'd receive an evasive reply, something to the effect neither was certain when this might be. But there in the yard sat the made-up train of cars, caboose attached! And the train might depart for Gunnison the next day!

Part of the deceit was based on the fact that passengers must be carried between Salida and Sargent, due to some old agreement. The railroad didn't want any passengers. Conductors couldn't accept cash fares, and you had to have a ticket. So for years I carried around tickets for the Sargent trip, never to be used.

Railfanning the Marshall Pass line was not easy. Chaffee County kept the gravel road open year-round for fishermen to reach a lake near Grays located west of Mears Junction. The road to the summit of the pass was an old trail, not maintained by anyone, following little Poncha Creek, so you ground along in second gear over large rocks and tree roots, branches scratching the paint of the car. All the way you were far below the track, unable to know if the train you sought to photograph was passing above you.

At the summit a half mile of meadow enabled the railroad to build a long siding, used to set out cars from doubling trains. The station and turntable were in a curving snowshed. Out the west side was an impressive view of mountains and valleys. Directly below, but four miles by track, was Shawano water tank and siding. If a train was coming from Gunnison, the smoke was visible for a good hour or more before it came into view at Shawano. If one were riding a train, traces of Otto Mears toll road could be seen here and there.

To get to Sargent and Gunnison, the fan would have to get back down to Poncha Junction, then drive west on U.S. 50. Sargent, until the K-36 and K-37 engines arrived, had a busy roundhouse. It still had a large coal dock like at Alamosa and a wye used frequently by train Helpers over the pass.

The rest of the line to Gunnison closely paralleled the highway, and this was true of the Baldwin and Crested Butte branches and partly so on the main to Montrose, with a gap of 15 miles when the railroad was in the depths of the Black Canyon, not emerging until Cimarron.

For those wanting to see the last remaining small engines of the D&RGW, Gunnison was the place, but most of the time they sat cold in the large roundhouse behind locked doors, no one around. After the aban-

ABOVE. For years at Salida on a Saturday close to Christmas, railroaders ran a "Santa Claus Train." A highly decorated caboose was taken to Poncha Junction where a local impersonator of the old gent would climb aboard, and the train would then stop at a street crossing where Santa would descend and lead the kids (and plenty of grownups too!) to a children's show at the nearby theater.

LEFT. Standard gauge switcher #1195 switches cabooses during preparations at Salida in December of 1950 for the annual Santa Claus train for the children of the city.

Santa Claus arrives by train from the North Pole at Salida on December 22, 1950.

Children of Salida pose with Santa after caboose #0578 has arrived, bringing him in supposedly from the North Pole, but actually, of course, only from Poncha Junction on December 22, 1950.

LEFT. Caboose #0589 is decorated for the last of the Santa Claus trains operated annually at Salida for the local children.

For the last time on December 22, 1950 #268 handles the Santa Claus train at Salida. It was brought up from Alamosa in one of the last trains on the Valley Line and was still in the yellow Grande Gold paint scheme it wore at the Chicago Railroad Fair in 1948-49. On both sides of the tender a color painting had been applied, lettered for the Cripple Creek & Tincup Railroad, an imaginary company. Sent to Gunnison, it handled the branch trains in this gaudy paint ensemble.

donment of the line beyond Sapinero through the Black Canyon in May of 1949, they were seldom found outside and under steam. The two C-21 outside-frame 2-8-0s might take a trip on the Sapinero Branch for some lumber shipments or go to Crested Butte once in a while. Such a snow plowing trip was fatal to #360. Trapped by a slush slide at Slate Cut, it froze up and was scrapped in 1950. The next year #361 also was sent to be scrapped.

That left but the two C-16 2-8-0s, and when the #268 went to the Chicago Railroad Fair in 1948, only the ancient and well-worn #278 was to inhabit that once busy roundhouse. It might sit cold for weeks before making a trip to either Baldwin or Sapinero. I'd watch the dispatcher's dope sheets for advance notice of these trips, and if I could get away that day, I would get an early start for the three-hour drive to Gunnison, perhaps only to find on arrival there that the trip had been postponed!

Unusual Rolling Stock

Gunnison also was home to some unusual rolling stock. It had the only wedge plow, a rock-loaded gondola with a huge locomotive-style plow topped by a headlight mounted on a sort of tower. It had the only "home-made" spreader on the system; #0524 was employed as a rolling home for the sectionmen. Apparently I was the only person to notice that caboose #0577 was erroneously lettered "Denver & Western Rio

Grande" on one side. The out-of-service B&B outfits consisted of old mail-express cars.

The former station, a modern construction of the 1920s, was to become Rio Grande Motorway headquarters and adjacent was a neat little board and batten building operated by the railroad as an eating house for crews, the woman operator living in quarters adjacent. Various non-revenue car bodies were overnight lodging for crews, and the section crew had been using the stone South Park depot along the Baldwin Branch.

For coaling there was the same kind of towering structure as used at Chama and Durango. The car shed had been a busy place, and its yard was composed of ancient rails dating to the 1880s, evidently original.

Three branches from Gunnison continued to be operated, rather irregularly. The Black Canyon abandonment of 1949 resulted in the stub to Sapinero becoming the branch of that name. Crested Butte was busy until Colorado Fuel & Iron closed down their big coal mine in 1952. The Baldwin Branch was the final 15 miles of what had originally been the final mileage of the Denver, South Park & Pacific and had steady though rather small shipments of household coal until the Valley Line to Alamosa was abandoned in 1951. On the Baldwin Branch due to a light bridge only the C-16 class engines could be used, which was fortunate for fans, as otherwise no C-16 would likely have survived.

Little C-16 2-8-0 #268 has pushed wedge snowplow #09271 as far as it could into a drift in the Gunnison Canyon and has left the balance of its train, consisting of a flanger and two cabooses in the distance, so it could get a run for the drifts. It was necessary to back the plow several times and wait for the section crew to clear the rails. At one point the Gunnison foreman vanished when he stepped into a culvert area, and he was hastily dug out by the section crew. This photo was taken on March 11, 1952.

Outside-frame Engine #360 is at Gunnison in 1945. The locomotive was dismantled in Salida on August 7, 1950. *Robert W. Richardson, collection of Mallory Hope Ferrell*

Class C-21 2-8-0 #361, an ex-Crystal River Railroad locomotive, switches at Gunnison in 1946. This locomotive, along with #360, served the Gunnison-Montrose line in its last years. This was a "little Mudhen." *Robert W. Richardson, collection of Mallory Hope Ferrell*

RATING OF LOCOMOTIVES IN TONS OF 2000 POUNDS
TONNAGE RATING SHOWN IN MINIMUM RATING

Number of tons of cars and lading in addition to engine and caboose which the different classes of engines will haul from and to the stations shown under favorable and unfavorable conditions.

"A" rating will be handled, except Superintendent may authorize either rating "B" or "C."

In computing tonnage, allowance will be made for excess cars on following basis: Divide the rating of engine or engines by 50, the quotient represents number of cars to be handled without frictional allowance. To each car in excess of quotient, add 4 tons. Illustration: Rating is 1250 tons, divide by 50 equals 25 cars, which is the rating of engine at 50 tons per car. To each car in excess of 25 add 4 tons to the stenciled or billed weight. In narrow gauge territory 2 1/2 tons friction will be used in computing weight of loads; to arrive at the number of cars that friction is to be figured on, 30 tons will be used. To illustrate: The combined rating out of Salida on 3 engines is 450 tons. Divide 450 by 30 which gives 15, friction to be figured at rate of 2 1/2 tons on each car on all cars in train over 15.

From	To	Engines Class 47 166 to 177 A	B	C	Engines Class 60 200 to 286 A	B	C	Engines Class 70 400 to 422 A	B	C	Engines Class 00 427 to 432 A	B	C	Engines Class 125 450 to 464 A	B	C
FIRST DISTRICT																
Salida	Poncha Jct.	105	95	85	190	170	150	230	210	185	260	235	210	350	315	280
Poncha Jct.	Mar. Pass or Pon. Pass	60	55	50	115	106	95	126	117	107	150	135	120	200	180	160
Marshall Pass	Buxton	575	575	575	575	575	575	800	800	800	800	800	800	800	800	800
Buxton	Gunnison															
Gunnison	Sargent	280	250	225	430	390	345	500	450	400	600	540	480	800	720	640
Sargent	Marshall Pass	60	55	50	115	106	95	126	117	107	150	135	120	200	180	160
Marshall Pass	Poncha Jct.	575	575	575	575	575	575	800	800	800	800	800	800	800	800	800
Poncha Jct.	Salida	900	900	900	900	900	900	1250	1250	1250	1250	1250	1250	1250	1250	1250
Poncha Jct.	Maysville	65	60	50	135	125	115	160	140	130	160	145	130	210	190	170
Maysville	Monarch	50	45	40	115	106	95	126	117	107	130	115	105	170	150	135
Monarch	Poncha Jct.	575	575	575	575	575	575	700	700	700	700	700	700	700	700	700
SECOND DISTRICT																
Gunnison	Crystal															
Crystal	Cimarron	240	215	190	380	340	305	440	395	350	530	475	405	700	630	560
Cimarron	Cerro	60	55	50	115	106	95	126	117	107	150	135	120	200	180	160
Cerro	Cedar Creek	575	575	575	575	575	575	800	800	800	800	800	800	800	800	800
Cedar Creek	Montrose	850	850	850	850	850	850	1200	1200	1200	1200	1200	1200	1200	1200	1200
Montrose	Ridgway	300	270	240	400	360	320	450	405	360	500	450	400	760	685	610
Ridgway	Ouray	150	135	120	240	215	190	260	235	210	275	250	225	400	360	320
Ouray	Ridgway	950	950	950	950	950	950	1300	1300	1300	1300	1300	1300	1300	1300	1300
Ridgway	Montrose															
Gunnison	Crested Butte	160	145	130	300	270	240	325	290	260	350	315	280	560	505	450
Crested Butte	Gunnison															
Sapinero	Lake City	200	180	160	325	295	260	350	315	280	375	340	300	580	520	460
THIRD DISTRICT																
Poncha Pass	Round Hill	800	800	800	800	800	800	1050	1050	1050	1050	1050	1050	1050	1050	1050
Round Hill	Alamosa															
Alamosa	Hot Springs	450	405	360	900	810	720	1000	900	800	1100	990	880	1350	1350	1350
Hot Springs	Villa Grove	425	385	335	725	655	580	800	720	640	900	810	720	1200	1080	960
Villa Grove	Round Hill	160	145	130	300	270	240	325	290	260	350	315	280	560	505	450
Round Hill	Poncha Pass	90	80	70	150	135	120	180	160	145	200	180	160	300	270	240
Poncha Pass	Poncha Jct.	575	575	575	575	575	575	800	800	800	800	800	800	800	800	800
Villa Grove	Orient	60	55	50	115	106	95	126	117	107	150	135	120	200	180	160
Orient	Villa Grove	575	575	575	575	575	575	800	800	800	800	800	800	800	800	800

ADDITIONAL SIDINGS AND SPURS NOT SHOWN IN REGULAR TIME TABLES

LOCATION District	Mile	NAMES	CAR CAPACITY SG	NG	SWITCH CONNECTIONS
First	215.47	West Salida	43	101	Both Ends.
"	250.80	Tank No. 7		12	West End.
"	254.33	Jackson Spur		7	East End.
"	262.94	Haig		7	East End.
"	285.91	Haverly		6	West End.
Second	292.49	Aberdeen Spur		2	East End.
"	297.13	Hall's Spur		3	East End.
"	342.51	Lu Jane		22	Both Ends.
"	343.45	West Portal		23	Both Ends.
"	357.25	Roe	5		Both Ends.
"	359.39	Frosts	9		East End.
"	364.69	Casner's	4		West End.
"	370.50	Sage	5		West End.
"	375.76	Campbell	7		West End.
Third	235.10	Alder		3	East End.
"	239.67	Davenport		7	East End.
"	291.13	Corlett		3	West End.
Monarch Branch	222.00	Charcoal		16	East End.
"	233.65	O. & C. Quarry		8	East End.
Crested Butte Br	289.24	Enders Spur		16	West End.
"	293.41	Hay Spur		5	East End.
"	297.09	Haymaker		2	East End.
"	298.83	Spring Creek		10	East End.
"	309.32	Bockers		3	East End.
"	311.29	Benton		7	East End.
"	314.87	Bulkley Jct.		23	East End.
"	315.59	Littell		24	East End.
"	318.48	Horace Mine		16	East End.
"	324.32	Irwin		3	East End.
Lake City Branch	334.79	Kellogs No. 1		3	East End.
"	337.63	Kellogs No. 2		3	East End.
"	333.00	Kellogs No. 3		3	East End.
Ouray Branch	385.41	Lotus		12	East End.
"	356.15	Vernal		8	East End.
"	369.03	Mayfield		6	East End.
"	373.84	Dallas Wye		34	Both Ends.
"	385.14	Wanika Smelter		20	East End.
"	385.24	Smelter		20	West End.
"	385.41	Lotus		12	East End.
"	379.41	Lewis		16	Both Ends.
North Fork Branch	374.00	Beet Track	25		Both Ends.
"	377.29	Saunders	8		Both Ends.
"	379.04	Read	11		East End.
"	400.48	Bell Creek	16		East End.
"	401.27	Elberta	10		East End.
"	401.35	Gibson	9		East End.
"	404.49	Hadleys	11		Both Ends.
"	407.16	Roberts	5		Both Ends.
"	408.00	Underwood	3		East End.
"	409.08	Morgan	2		Both Ends.
"	412.03	Juanita Junc.	50		West End.
"	416.11	Coal Mines	233		East End.
Baldwin Branch	292.57	Vidals Spur		2	East End.
"	299.00	Lehmans Spur		2	East End.
"	305.00	Wallace Spur		6	East End.
"	305.84	Green Canon		33	West End.
Pitkin Branch	289.24	Bank		3	West End.
"	290.17	Ashley		4	East End.

Charts taken from Employees' Time Table in effect March 28, 1920.

Beginning at Poncha Junction, the Monarch Branch was the busiest of all the remaining narrow gauge lines until it was standard gauged in 1956, often seeing two 52-car trains of gondolas on the same day.

So the Gunnison lines of the old Third Division had a lot of interest and variety of operations, but in 1948 I didn't expect that it would vanish so quickly in the next few years.

Mears Junction

Eleven miles west of Salida on the 4% grade to Marshall Pass, the toll roads of Otto Mears and ex-Governor Gilpin joined, and a small community grew up consisting of several business buildings and a scattering of homes. Gilpin had built a toll road from the south over Poncha Pass to handle wheat traffic and other farm products intended for the booming Leadville area in the late 1870s. Mears had built his toll road leading to Gunnison. Both toll companies were taken over by the D&RG and were used to a great extent in the railroad's construction in 1880-1881.

The resulting track configuration at Mears Junction looked more like something invented for a model rail layout than for a three-foot-gauge railroad. The main line was a tangent, and to get started on the 3.6-mile climb to Poncha Pass, the line took off using a half circle loop to cross over the Gunnison main line on a trestle and head up to the pass. Track facilities were meager—a passing track, a stub end spur and a water tank. And evidently, in the early days, there was a station with a telegraph operator.

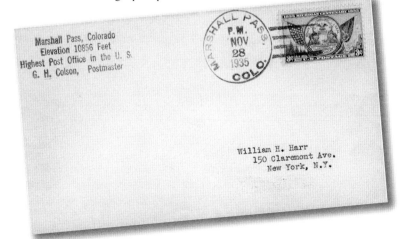

The year-round population of Marshall Pass included not only the telegraph operator, but a section crew, car inspector and often other employees. Also in residence was a man who looked after water rights and accompanying ditches; he was also the postmaster. In the days of passenger trains many postcards were mailed to get the "cachet" applied, stating this was the highest post office in the U.S. With discontinuance of passenger trains in November of 1940, the post office was also closed.

ADJUSTED TONNAGE RATINGS

From	To	Tons	Tons	Tons	Tons	Tons	Tons	Tons	Tons	Tons
Salida	Tennessee Pass	3300	2230	2330	1800	1600	1210	1070	940	4
Minturn	Tennessee Pass	1400	950	1000	780	685	550	450	420	2

From	To	Class of Engine K-36 No. of Engines 480-489	Class of Engine K-28 No. of Engines 470-479	Class of Engine K-27 No. of Engines 450-464	Class of Engine C-25 No. of Engines 375	Class of Engine C-21 No. of Engines 360, 361	Class of Engine C-17, C-18 No. of Engines 300-320	Class of Engine C-19 No. of Engines 340-349	Class of Engine C-16 No. of Engines 200-286	Adjustment Factors
		Tons	Tons	Tons	Tons	Tons	Tons	Tons	Tons	Tons
Poncha Junction	Marshall Pass	232	187	183	173	113	106	92	79	1
Buxton	Marshall Pass	232	187	183	173	113	106	92	79	1
Poncha Junction	Mayville						120	105	89	2
Maysville	Monarch						88	75	65	1
Mears Junction	Poncha Pass	232	187	183	173	113	106	92	79	1
Alamosa	Moffat-both ways	2950	2220	2030	2000	1560	1190	1190	1120	12
Mineral Hot Springs	Villa Grove	1650	1250	1135	1135	920	660	675	630	7
Moffat	Mineral Hot Springs	1200	915	830	830	600	480	480	420	5
Villa Grove	Round Hill	700	570	520	520	380	300	300	270	3
Round Hill	Poncha Pass	360	280	275	250	175	160	140	120	2
Villa Grove	Orient						106	92	79	1
Orient	Villa Grove						460	460	440	5
Moffat	Crestone								295	4
Gunnison	Sargent	1430	1000	950	875	625	555	505	450	5
Parlin	Pitkin						145	120	110	2
Gunnison	Crested Butte		660	630	570	410	360	340	290	4
Crested Butte	Floresta		300	290	275	190	170	150	130	2
Gunnison	Castleton						270	240	210	4
Castleton	Baldwin						180	155	140	3
Crystal Creek	Cerro Summit			183			106	92	79	1
Montrose	Cerro Summit			183			106	92	79	1
Crystal Creek	Gunnison						570	520	465	5
Sapinero	Lake City						295	260	225	4
Montrose	Ridgway			790			460	420	370	5
Ridgway	Ouray			390			230	205	180	3

These ratings are the usual tonnage ratings for dead freight trains. Chief Dispatchers are authorized to increase or decrease these ratings in their discretion in accordance with standing instructions, to adjust for slack grades, condition of power, necessity for maintaining stock schedules, or for any other reasons which justify.

In computing tonnage, the adjustment factor represents the number of Tons which shall be added to the total weight of each car, loaded or empty. The caboose shall count as a car. Tonnage hauled may exceed the rating by a fraction of a car.

On 4% grades, engines equipped with
1-9½" Compressor 30 Cars 575 Tons
1-11" Compressor 45 Cars 650 Tons
2-9½" Compressor 60 Cars 800 Tons
When equipped with one 8 1/2" C.C. air Compressor,
35 cars coal or other heavy loading 1150 tons
45 cars stock and other light loading 1150 tons
45 cars mixed loads and empties 1150 tons
60 cars empties 1150 tons
150 tons additional may be handled Shirley to Mears Jct.
Poncha Jct. to Salida and Buxton to Sargent
100 Cars—2000 tons
Monarch to Maysville 500 tons.

Salida Division, June 12, 1927

THIRD DIVISION
SECOND DISTRICT
Salida and Gunnison

WESTWARD — THIRD CLASS / SECOND CLASS / FIRST CLASS   **EASTWARD** — FIRST CLASS / SECOND CLASS / THIRD CLASS

Time Table No. 100 — March 28, 1920

327 Freight (Leave Daily Exc. Sunday)	323 Freight (Leave Tues, Thurs, and Saturday)	351 Pitkin Mixed (Leave Mon, Wed, and Friday)	331 Monarch Mixed (Leave Tuesday and Saturday)	317 Denver, Alamosa and Durango Passenger (Leave Daily Exc. Sunday)	315 Marshall Pass Route Express (Leave Daily)	Distance from Denver	STATIONS	Distance from Gunnison	Passing Tracks (Siding Capacity in Cars)	316 Marshall Pass Route Express (Arrive Daily)	318 Denver, Alamosa and Durango Passenger (Arrive Daily Exc. Sunday)	332 Monarch Mixed (Arrive Tuesday and Saturday)	352 Pitkin Mixed (Arrive Mon, Wed and Friday)	324 Freight (Arrive Mon, Wed and Friday)	328 Freight (Arrive Daily Exc. Sunday)
7.30 AM	8.20 AM		7.10 AM	4.10 PM	6.00 AM	215.11	S SALIDA RNWCYT (4.99)	73.53	Yard	9.30 PM	12.05 PM	4.00 PM		5.00 PM	6.00 PM
7.55	8.50		7.45 AM	f 4.25 324	f 6.15	220.10	PONCHA JC. Y (3.75)	68.54	56	f 9.15	f 11.51	3.15 AM		f 4.25 317	5.30
8.25	9.15			4.35	f 6.29	223.85	OTTO (2.17)	64.79	28	f 9.01	11.35			4.00	5.05
8.50	9.40 AM			4.50 PM 328	s 6.40	226.02	MEARS JC. RWCY (2.30)	62.62	32	s 8.53	11.26 AM			3.36 PM	4.50 317
9.10					f 6.50	228.32	SHIRLEY W (3.62)	60.32	33	f 8.44					4.20
9.40					f 7.08	231.94	KEENE (2.06)	56.70	15	f 8.30					3.55
10.00					f 7.20	234.00	GRAY'S WC (3.57)	54.64	43	f 8.22					3.40
10.30					f 7.38	237.57	POCONO (3.14)	51.07	20	f 8.08					3.15
11.30					s 8.00 / 8.05	240.71	Mp MARSHALL PASS RNWCT (4.14)	47.93	36	s 7.55 / 7.50					2.50
12.05 PM					f 8.20	244.85	SHAWANO W (3.66)	43.79	35	f 7.24					1.30
12.50 328					f 8.33	248.51	CHESTER (4.24)	40.13	28	f 7.04					12.50 327
1.20					f 8.48	252.75	BUXTON (4.49)	35.89	45	f 6.44					12.10 PM
2.20					s 9.05	257.24	Sj SARGENT RDWCYT (4.81)	31.40	115	s 6.31					11.20
2.50					f 9.17	262.05	ELKO (3.43)	26.59	45	f 6.13					10.30
3.05					f 9.25	265.48	CROOKTON W (3.98)	23.16	22	f 6.03					10.10
3.20					s 9.34	269.46	DOYLE (0.93)	19.18	18	s 5.53					9.45
3.25					9.37 328	270.39	BONITA (6.43)	18.25	43	5.50					9.37 315
3.55		1.45 PM			s 9.54 352	276.82	PARLIN W (5.34)	11.82	27	s 5.34			9.54 AM 315		8.45
4.15		2.05			f 10.07	282.16	STEELE (6.48)	6.48	41	f 5.21			9.15		8.15
							Gu-Di GUNNISON RNWCYT								
4.50 PM		2.30 PM			10.25 AM	288.64	(73.53)		Yard	5.05 PM			8.55 AM		7.45 AM
Arrive Daily Exc. Sunday	Arrive Tues, Thurs, and Saturday	Arrive Mon, Wed, Friday	Arrive Tuesday and Saturday	Arrive Daily Exc. Sunday	Arrive Daily		....Time Over District.... / ...Average Miles Per Hour...			Leave Daily	Leave Daily Exc. Sunday	Leave Tuesday and Saturday	Leave Mon, Wed, and Friday	Leave Mon, Wed, and Friday	Leave Daily Exc. Sunday
(9.20) 7.87	(1.20) 8.18	(.45) 15.76	(.35) 8.55	(.40) 16.36	(4.25) 16.64					(4.25) 16.64	(.39) 16.78	(.45) 6.65	(.59) 12.02	(1.24) 7.79	(10.15) 7.17

SPECIAL INSTRUCTIONS

A-1. EASTWARD TRAINS ARE SUPERIOR TO WESTWARD TRAINS OF THE SAME CLASS.

A-2. No train will leave Salida, Marshall Pass, Sargent or Gunnison without clearance.

A-3. Water tanks 2.0 miles east of Buxton and MP 239.5.

A-4. All trains must stop at Marshall Pass for inspection of train and brakes.

A-5. Passenger trains will not exceed a speed of 15 miles per hour and freight trains 10 miles per hour down grade between Marshall Pass and Tank 7 MP 250.84 and between Marshall Pass and Poncha Junction.

A-6. Eastward freight trains will stop 10 minutes at Mears Junction, and westward freight trains will stop 10 minutes at Chester to cool wheels and inspect train.

A-7. Telegraphones located Poncha Jct., Mears Jct., Gray's, Marshall Pass, Shawano, Chester, Buxton, Sargent, Elko, Crookton, Doyle and Parlin.

A-8. Haig, at MP 262.94, is flag stop for Nos. 315 and 316.

Locomotive #361 arrives at Gunnison with a stock train from Cimarron on September 17, 1946, before the line through the Black Canyon was abandoned in 1949. A contract for the D&RG line between Salida and Gunnison over Marshall Pass was let in September, 1880, and the railroad reached Gunnison on August 6, 1881. *Robert W. Richardson, collection of Mallory Hope Ferrell*

D&RGW #268 in "bumblebee" colors blackens the blue Colorado sky as it nears Gunnison from Iola with a stock extra on October 9, 1953. The 2-8-0 locomotive displays a sleeve-type cinder catcher that was used briefly by the railroad. *Robert W. Richardson, collection of Mallory Hope Ferrell*

Westbound trains to Gunnison usually consisted of empty gondolas for coal loading at Crested Butte. This is a typical three-engine train making the climb from Poncha Junction with the second engine in the middle of the train and the third ahead of the caboose. Locomotives #497, #499 and #493 are shown on March 13, 1950 rounding a bend through the mountains.

As the Poncha Pass trains often had to double or triple the hill, an unusual short piece of track was employed to create the equivalent of a wye. There was a track connection from the south side of the loop to a switch a few hundred feet west on the main line. Locomotives could use this track, back down the main, and then they were headed correct for the next "double."

From the 1880s through the 1920s, the Poncha Pass line was fairly busy, bringing iron ore from the Orient Mine at the north end of the San Luis Valley. Then in 1890 track was completed beyond that junction to Alamosa, 55 miles to the south, most of it tangent, resulting in the 74-mile line from Mears to Alamosa, which had a 53-mile tangent, one of the longest in the U.S. For the first 10 years or so, trains that heretofore reached Alamosa via La Veta were instead routed via Mears, so the new Valley Line was busy with freight and passenger traffic.

Completion in 1899 of a new standard gauge line into Alamosa ended much of this traffic, and the iron traffic continued heavy until about 1928 when a disaster closed it. After that, trains only ran to Alamosa about once a month, until abandonment in February of 1951.

The Valley Line

The San Luis Valley Branch, as it was officially named, was an unusual narrow gauge line. Its trackage, at elevation of 7,500 feet, was completed in 1890. It was an extension of the line built in 1881 from Mears Junction on the main line to Gunnison, over Poncha Pass to Villa Grove and ending at Orient at the iron mine of the Colorado Coal & Iron Co.

So from a junction at Villa Grove, track crews had an easy time building the line at the rate of a mile a day, using secondhand 45-pound rail, untreated ties and no ballast. Because the area only received about six

After making a deal to purchase the siding signs on the abandoned Marshall Pass route, the problem was how to get them, as most were long distances from any road or trail. The Brinkerhoff Brothers loaned a motorcar and this eased the task. Pocono was the last siding before the summit. It is July 22, 1955 and after a couple of months the track was gone and eventually the county made a road out of the grade.

inches of moisture a year, ballasting was no problem, and the line remained essentially as built until it was torn up in 1951.

There was a little traffic from points along the new line, and a little farming, but much of it was discouraged by the heavy alkali nature of the soil. But the line did serve as a connection between the two narrow gauge divisions. Passenger trains now were routed to Salida instead of via La Veta Pass, and Durango trains used the Valley Line. This arrangement lasted until the new standard gauge line over La Veta Pass was completed in 1899. For a decade the Valley Line was busy.

But after that decade, a two-car passenger train made the Alamosa to Salida roundtrip and usually a mixed train as well. The passenger train lasted until 1927; it was headed by a T-12 with the RPO-express car and a single coach. A mixed train operated briefly on the 17-mile Crestone Branch which began at Moffat. The gold mine at the end of

track was plagued by immense amounts of water and operated only sporadically.

A trip on the mixed train must have been about the most boring train trip in Colorado, with that seemingly endless tangent; even if on schedule it took eight hours for the 100-mile run from Salida. And, of course, there might be several hours added while the crew made a side trip to Crestone. The passenger train made the trip in four hours, making it the fastest trip by narrow gauge to be found on the D&RG.

Until 1942, ore traffic from the Orient Branch supplied a lot of traffic, and early in this century the Mudhen 2-8-2 type engines were busy with three-engine trains to Poncha Pass. Before their advent, all of the Class C-19 2-8-0s were kept busy with this and Marshall Pass traffic.

A growing farming output just west of the line from Mosca and Hooper resulted in a third rail being added in 1928 to handle that traffic. Idler

In 1950 one large mill was still processing ore at Silverton, so the scheduled mixed train from Durango included box cars for that loading, as seen on August 12, 1950. Train #461 operated three times a week, and as tourism increased, eventually the train was a daily affair in the summer. *Clayton Tanner*

The railroad reached Durango, named because it resembled the terrain around Durango, Mexico, in 1881. As shown, Durango's Main Street in 1950 is quiet in the early morning before the daily departure of the Silverton Mixed. The boom was yet to come from the gas and oil drillings in the San Juan Basin. *Clayton Tanner*

When snow got deep and slides ran on the Silverton Branch, selected engines of the Mudhen Class were equipped with these huge pilots. In the background is Engine #463 ready for a trip, the crew having learned that although there wasn't any snow in Durango, they could expect slides in the last few miles into 9,300-foot-high Silverton. The plow in the foreground appears to be the one reserved for Rio Grande Southern Engine #42. *Clayton Tanner*

The Durango roundhouse crew equipped the #463 Mudhen with its large plow in readiness for winter slides, even though the date is August, 1950 and it's still warm weather. Summer was the time to work on snowfighting equipment, flangers, pilots and rotaries. *Clayton Tanner*

OPPOSITE TOP. Business car *Nomad* was the former B-3 of the D&RGW and was sold in 1951 to a private party. The third set of owners was intrigued by Lucius Beebe's tall tale in books about a car of this name allegedly used by General William Palmer, so they named the B-3 *Nomad*. It is now used by charter parties on the Durango & Silverton Railroad. This picture shows the car on August 9, 1972. *Clayton Tanner*

The coaling structure at Durango, shown in 1950, was duplicated at Chama and Gunnison, but only the Chama coaling tower survives today. Class C-18 locomotive #319 was the switch engine at Durango and was frequently rented to the RGS. It was scrapped the next year after being used in the staged head-on collision for the movie *Denver & Rio Grande*. *Clayton Tanner*

OPPOSITE BOTTOM. The United States Army designed and built this experimental diesel intended to be used on gauges up to 42" by making simple changes in the trucks. It was tested in 1959 on the lines out of Alamosa, and eventually, as shown here, was used at Durango on both Farmington and Silverton trains. It was found that the Army-designed trucks were too rigid, and when it was first tried out, the #3000 frequently derailed. *Lee Monroe*

Diesel #50 was the only narrow gauge diesel on the D&RGW. Built by Davenport-Besler in 1937 for an Oregon lumber firm, it became the switcher at Baker for the Sumpter Valley Ry. It was purchased by the D&RGW in 1963 to replace the steam switch engine used at Durango. By changing trackage at Durango, and with freights no longer handled at Durango, there wasn't any need for a switch engine, and it was sold in 1970 to the Roaring Camp & Big Trees tourist line at Felton, California. It was heavily damaged in a runaway, sold in 1981 to the Durango Railroad Museum (Bob Shank, Jr.) and now is being restored at the Colorado Railroad Museum in Golden. This photograph was taken in Durango in July of 1964. *Clayton Tanner*

The engineer looks for a highball at Chama while piloting an Illini Railroad Club special in June of 1959. The club sponsored a special train on the Burlington that departed from Chicago. The #476 was put through the shop at Alamosa and emerged with a fresh coat of paint. *Lee Monroe*

This is a typical summertime Durango & Silverton Narrow Gauge Railroad train headed by a Class K-36 leaving Durango in June of 1992. Increasingly, as the years have gone by, the D&S relies on these heavier class engines. *Lee Monroe*

The "Grande Gold" paint of 1950 didn't survive much shopping as the mechanical force gradually replaced it with black, and removed the box headlight as well. The odd stack, however, remained on the engine and its sisters until Charles Bradshaw, Jr. bought the Silverton line in 1981 and had the dummy stacks removed. *Lee Monroe*

In winding its way up the Animas Valley, despite a long train, the engine on the Silverton train of 1950 often was out of sight of passengers. The tracks near Durango often were flooded in spring due to a rapid snow melt in the mountains. The railroad follows the course of the Animas River or River of the Lost Souls all the way to the picturesque former mining town of Silverton. *Clayton Tanner*

OPPOSITE. A favorite spot for camera fans is where U.S. 550 crosses over the Silverton Branch about 16 miles north of Durango station. In another mile the railroad passes through Rockwood and then enters the canyon by passing around the High Line above the river. Class K-37 #497 was used for a while but proved too heavy for the line and was traded to the Cumbres & Toltec Scenic for a K-36 Class engine. *Lee Monroe*

At Hermosa the Valley of the Animas narrows and the locomotive commences a stiff climb for a few miles before reaching Rockwood. The ruling grade on the branch is 2.5%, and in good weather a Class K-28 can handle 10-car trains. This photograph was taken on July 26, 1950. *Clayton Tanner*

The ill-fated *Silver Vista* had a glass roof and large side windows. During much of the trip passengers abandoned their reserved seats to crowd onto the narrow rear platform to enjoy the scenery. This was the scene at Rockwood on July 26, 1950, and in a few minutes those seats would be empty, as the train crawled around the High Line, some 300 feet above the river. *Clayton Tanner*

It earned the nickname "The Painted Train" by locals when Engine #473, the combine and three open platform coaches were painted "Grande Gold." It had been running less than a couple of months when it was photographed on July 26, 1950 with the engine and cars bright and clean. As a mixed train, it carried the caboose for the crew, but a group of bridge players from a dude ranch preferred the caboose for the entire trip. *Clayton Tanner*

The Mechanical Department only reluctantly agreed to have the #473 painted "Grande Gold," and most of this fancy paint job vanished by the next year or two. This treatment of the engine and the five remaining open platform cars was said to have been done at the insistence of Harold F. Eno, the passenger traffic manager, and he used his department's budget to pay for the extra cost. Alfred Perlman, the road's executive, was away advising Israel on its railroad problems, and upon his return was outraged at this, but Eno was upheld by President Wilson McCarthy. *Clayton Tanner*

BELOW. In Gunnison Canyon little C-16 #268, last of its kind in operation, moves the final Powderhorn-by-rail roundup train from Iola to Gunnison in October of 1953. Each fall ranchers of the Powderhorn area gathered their stock, and amid a community party, had a good time preparing the shipments. This track was part of the original main line of the D&RG, which west of Iola ran through the Black Canyon and on to Montrose. *Clayton Tanner*

LEFT. In Silverton the tracks were eventually extended to within a block of the main street, a project of Alexis McKinney during his three years tenure as head of the Rio Grande Land Co. when the D&RGW upgraded the line after losing an abandonment application. It was just one of many improvements he developed. This photo was taken in July of 1975. *Donald J. Heimburger*

In Cimarron Canyon where the old main line left the Black Canyon, the National Park Service arranged to display C-16 #278 with a box car and caboose on an original bridge. The #278 had been retired in 1952 and given to Montrose, but after it was heavily vandalized, it was placed here where it was much safer from such attention. A stock yard and some freight cars have been reconstructed and added to the display. Cimarron was a regular stop for its eating house and was at the foot of the 4% grade to Cerro Summit. *Lee Monroe*

Now a county museum, the D&RGW depot in Montrose was a busy place for passenger mail and express traffic. Here the tracks were three-rail, and passengers changed from one gauge train to another. Now the end of the line from Grand Junction, in earlier times the station hosted trains to Salida and Ouray and much traffic to and from the Rio Grande Southern. *Clayton Tanner*

After a trip to Monarch or Marshall Pass it was the duty of Salida hostlers to hose down the locomotives. After a roundtrip the running boards were inches deep in cinders. Arthur W. Wallace took this photo in 1955.

D&RGW's Baldwin C-16 2-8-0 #268 with a cabbage stack appears in her Grande Gold "make-up" at the west edge of Gunnison on U.S. Highway #50 in July of 1962. The #268, the *Montezuma*, hauled the last revenue train west of Gunnison. *Clayton Tanner*

D&RGW #480, a 1925 K-36 Baldwin, leads an eastbound approaching the Marshall snowsheds on October 6, 1951. *Robert W. Richardson, collection of Mallory Hope Ferrell*

A "double double" stock train (four locomotives) makes a run for the Pass on the Sargent to Marshall Pass line on September 11, 1953. This was the next to last four-locomotive stock train run on the line. *Robert W. Richardson, collection on Mallory Hope Ferrell*

Blasting up Marshall Pass with a train of gondolas in the fall of 1951, #483 and #481 are eastbound near the summit. Locomotive #480 brings up the rear of the train, seen behind the tall pine trees to the left. *Robert W. Richardson, collection of Mallory Hope Ferrell*

TOP. A four-engine stock extra pounds the iron as it climbs Marshall Pass on October 9, 1953 with Powderhorn cattle. The last four-engine train, with locomotives #489, #483, #482 and #480, are near Sargent. *Robert W. Richardson, collection of Mallory Hope Ferrell*

BOTTOM. A clean-up train of stock empties heads up Marshall Pass on September 10, 1953. Engine #483 is in the lead, with #489 helping on the rear. It's likely the aspens are beginning to turn golden yellow about this time of year. *Robert W. Richardson, collection of Mallory Hope Ferrell*

A Crested Butte coal freight with #480 pushing, and three other locomotives ahead of it, lift tonnage over Marshall Pass in 1951. *Robert W. Richardson, collection of Mallory Hope Ferrell*

Engine #489 emerges from the east portal of the Marshall Pass snowshed in 1954. After abandonment in 1955 the shed was removed, and the station building, as well as others connected to the snowshed, were torn down. It is now simply a curving cut on the cindered byway.

For almost the last time, a locomotive takes water at Sargent. The #489 was used by the dismantlers and would complete its work over Marshall Pass later during September of 1955. Track was removed as far as Poncha Junction; the tank still stands at Sargent.

cars were carried on all freights in both directions between Hooper and Alamosa.

Under the old Third Division the Valley Line was part of it, and Salida crews had the rights on the branch. Only in an emergency could a crew from Alamosa operate over the branch. One time in 1909 the fireman became ill, and a fireman residing at Alamosa was drafted to take his place. To his surprise the engine that came in from Salida wasn't a D&RG engine but instead was Florence & Cripple Creek Railroad 2-8-0 #8. The Third Division was short of power, and for a while rented a number of idle engines from the F&CC.

The Alamosa man told me that many years later he got to operate the same engine on a trip over Cumbres Pass, though now it belonged to the D&RGW and was numbered #318.

In 1951 the line from Hooper to Mears Junction was abandoned, but the remaining 20 miles to Alamosa was still operated by crews from Salida. They were paid one day for coming to Alamosa to get their train, one day for the 40-mile roundtrip to Hooper and a third day's pay to return to Salida. It cost 50% more in payroll to run the 20-mile stub than it did to make the roundtrip from Salida to Alamosa. It was just one of those strange things as a result of old railroad contracts.

The abandonment and the last run from Alamosa was on February 15, 1951. The last train consisted of two box cars and caboose north of Hooper, where idlers and standard gauge reefers had been set out.

Last Run on the Valley Line

Even the train crew of the last train from Salida to Alamosa didn't know when leaving the Salida yard that theirs was indeed the last run. The railroad received ICC permission the year before and was very secretive of its intentions. By the time the last train arrived to take water at Mears Junction, the trainmaster told the conductor this was the last run: February 14, 1951.

No notices to the public were to be seen anywhere along the line, though they were posted inside the two locked up depots at Moffat and Hooper, presumably for the information of resident mice. Storekeepers at two points were expecting each a car of Baldwin coal, several of which were in the train, but, again, without notice or explanation, the cars went on through to Alamosa consignees.

At Hooper, beginning of the three-rail trackage, the odd idler car unique to the branch was picked up. This was an old engine tender, fitted with three-way couplers. When smaller engines had been used on the branch, it was hauled northbound full of water and used as a "tank" at Hooper. The K-36 and K-37 classes of Mikados, however, had ample water, so in the final years the idler car was hauled "dry." If an engine did need water further north, in an emergency it could draw on an artesian well at each point, which didn't have the large stream a regular tank would supply.

The return trip north on the next day on February 15 included four empty standard gauge refrigerators to leave at Hooper and some empty gondolas for the scrappers, so that beyond Moffat the train had only two box cars and a caboose. There was little snow on the route, only a few inches on the pass, so the big plow pilot of #482 wasn't really needed. And thus a second break was made in the famed Narrow Gauge Circle.

Gunnison—Long Time Important Division Point

From 1882 when the new D&RG main line was opened, Gunnison was an important division point, headquarters for many crews, and an important roundhouse point. At first the railroad designated this as the Fourth Division. The First was from Denver to Pueblo, the Second was beyond that to Leadville, and the Third was centered at Alamosa. In the 1890s in a shuffle of the type railroads liked to do, to confuse their own people as well as outsiders, the Third and Fourth divisions exchanged designations, which they kept until 1923 when in another shuffle of divisions, management gave names to the various divisions.

The Third Division became a storied operation, helped along by numerous articles and references in *Railroad Stories* and *Railroad Man's* magazines. Originally it encompassed the main line from Salida via Gunnison to Grand Junction, with the numerous branches such as that to Ouray, Crested Butte, North Fork, Monarch and the San Luis Valley. Through traffic had vanished with the opening in 1890 of the new standard gauge line west of Salida via Glenwood Springs to Grand Junction and on to Utah via the Rio Grande Western Railway.

But the Third Division remained very busy with a good variety of traffic, strong in coal and other mining products, forest products and, of course, cattle and sheep.

When heavier engines came to the railroad, they went to the Third Division, as in 1881 the dozen Class 70s (later C-19), the half dozen Class 71s (later C-17) in 1887 and in 1903 the 15 Class 125 2-8-2s (later K27).

Even during World War I the acquisition of secondhand power from the Florence & Cripple Creek and Crystal River railroads went first to the Third Division. The relative importance of the two narrow gauge divisions was shown by the first Class 70 engines not appearing on the Fourth Division until they were some 20 years old, in 1903! And the famed "Mudhen" (Class 125) didn't get to the Fourth Division until 1914, and then only for use on the Cumbres Helper District.

Major track improvements were made to Marshall Pass, filling in wooden trestles and easing the sharper curves in a number of places, lengthening sidings, installing a covered turntable at the summit, etc. This kind of improvement budgeting never reached Cumbres Pass.

DENVER AND RIO GRANDE RAILWAY.
ANNUAL PASS.
NARROW GAUGE.

PASS Mr. J. L. Sanderson
On Account of Southern Overland Mail Co

Upon the Conditions on the back of this Ticket, until December 31st, 1872, unless otherwise ordered.

Wm J Palmer
President.

No. 86

D & R G W Form 3250
Sec. 8 Page 81
D & S L Form 1196

Alamosa Sept 6th

TRAIN ORDER No. 27

To C&E Engs 456 and 463

At Montrose ___ X ___ Opr. ___ M.

Engs 456 and 463 run as 1 extra Montrose to Cerro Summit and return as 2 extra Cerro Summit to Montrose

L.S.L.
Chief Dispatcher

CONDUCTOR, ENGINEMAN AND REAR TRAINMAN MUST EACH HAVE A COPY OF THIS ORDER

Made Cm Time 616 PM Cowan Opr.

OPPOSITE RIGHT. A September 15, 1948 excursion has halted at the Sargent tank. The depot had closed several years earlier. The return trip from Gunnison was made at night in the moonlight, amid the fall colors which were at their height. The little depot was moved to Gunnison by the historical society and is their railroad museum.

Engine #489 in from Marshall Pass and now at Poncha Junction is in a spring snowstorm on April 8, 1950. The small amount of snow on the plow indicates that little snow had been encountered on the pass. When an operator had been stationed here during WWII and earlier, the large number of trains passing this point required the use of the semaphore, nearly the only one to be found on the narrow gauge.

With standard gauging of the Monarch Branch, there wasn't any more narrow gauge at Salida, and the cars and engines were brought to Alamosa on standard gauge cars, as in this December 14, 1955 picture. The Car Department had a sturdy wooden movable ramp that could be fitted against the end of the standard gauge car and the cars rolled down.

THIRD DIVISION
MONARCH BRANCH
Poncha Junction and Monarch

Westward SECOND CLASS 331 Monarch Mixed Leave Tues. & Sat.	Distance from Denver		Time Table No. 100 March 28, 1920 STATIONS		Distance from Monarch	Siding Capacity in Cars Passing Tracks	Eastward SECOND CLASS 332 Monarch Mixed Arrive Tues. & Sat
7.45 AM	220.10	Gu	PONCHA JUNC.	Y	15.30	56	3.15 PM
			6.91				
8.35	227.01		MAYSVILLE		8.39	21	1.45
			5.98				
9.40	232.99		GARFIELD		2.41	22	12.45 AM
			2.41				
11.20 AM	235.40		MONARCH	T		21	11.45 AM
Arrive Tues. & Sat		Be	(15.30)				Leave Tues. & Sat
(3.35)			........Time Over District.......				(3.30)
4.27			....Average Miles Per Hour....				4.37

G-1. EASTWARD TRAINS ARE SUPERIOR TO WESTWARD TRAINS OF THE SAME CLASS.

G-2. Water Tank at Silver Creek, between Maysville and Garfield.

G-3. No. 332 will wait at Monarch until No. 331 arrives.

Management often discussed standard gauging the narrow gauge lines, especially the Third Division, which at times became a traffic bottleneck. But all the talk amounted to just standard gauging the lines from Grand Junction to Montrose and the North Fork Branch from Delta in 1907.

The savings in standard gauging were tempting, but the D&RG never seemed to be able to find the dollars; it was hard enough to pay fixed debts and maintain its standard gauge main lines. There just wasn't any money for the narrow gauges. So they had to make do with old engines and obsolete cars, both freight and passenger.

The 1890 new main line enabled selling off all the smaller engines, including the 4-4-0s, and by 1916 they got rid of the last of the smallest and oldest Class 56 2-8-0s. The 4-6-0 released from the main line now powered passenger trains on both the Third and Fourth divisions.

By 1914 some of the 2-8-2 Mudhens were spared to work the Cumbres hill turns out of Chama, the only stretch of track on that division suitable for the heavier engines. Not until heavier rail was laid from Antonito to Durango, secondhand from a standard gauge rail change, but very good 70# steel, could the Mudhens work the entire Fourth Division main line.

Although heavier rail had been laid from Sargent to Ridgway and to Crested Butte, the Mudhens had such close clearances they were banned from use through the Black Canyon to Cimarron. The secondhand engines received in 1916-1917 had therefore dominated the Gunnison-Montrose-Ridgway trackage. The two smaller Crystal River locomotives largely held down the Gunnison westerly runs. But their wide tires kept them from going on to Ouray and being used on the RGS. So the ex-F&CC engines handled much of the work on that portion.

Until the Class K-28 2-8-2 #470-479 engines arrived in 1923, many of the hill turns on Marshall Pass were accomplished by mixtures of K-27 and smaller engines, including many C-16s, and the C-21 Crystal River engines, except during winter snows. Again, with their wide tires they proved unsuitable with other engines when the snow was heavy.

Crested Butte Branch

Little attention has been paid the Crested Butte Branch, even though it provided a great amount of coal traffic that kept the lines into the Gunnison area in existence. When the last big coal mine at Crested Butte closed in 1952, abandonment of those lines soon followed.

For most of its 29 miles, the branch was in open ranch country following the Slate River on an easy grade on which a single K-36 or K-37 could move a long train of empty gondolas. The town was at an elevation

A Monarch Branch train enters Salida yard at the point where the third rail for standard gauge ended. This was a busy branch for most of the year, the trains bringing in 52 heavily-loaded cars of limestone at a time.

Denver, Colorado Springs and Pueblo to Gunnison, Montrose and Grand Junction via Marshall Pass

Read down				Read up
No. 315 Daily	Miles from Denver	STATIONS NARROW GAUGE 5-19-12		No. 316 Daily
9 00	0.0	lv .... Denver Union Depot ...... ar		7 40
11 48	74.9	lv .... Colorado Springs .... ar		4 40
1 05	119.4	ar .... Pueblo Union Depot lv		3 15
1 15	119.4	lv .... Pueblo Union Depot ..... ar		2 55
5 15	215.1	ar .... Salida lv		**11 15**
6 30	215.1	lv .... Salida .... ar		**8 45**
6 45	220.1	.... Poncha Junction		**8 21**
....	223.9	.... Otto		....
7 10	226.0	.... Mears Junction		**8 00**
f 7 20	228.3	.... Shirley		f 7 52
....	231.9	.... Keene		....
f 7 50	234.0	.... Gray's		f 7 33
....	237.6	.... Pocono		....
8 29	240.7	ar .... Marshall Pass lv		7 10
8 35	240.7	lv .... Marshall Pass .... ar		7 05
f 8 50	244.9	.... Shawano		f 6 38
f 9 03	248.5	.... Chester		f 6 18
....	252.8	.... Buxton		....
9 35	257.2	ar .... Sargent lv		5 45
9 35	257.2	lv .... Sargent .... ar		5 45
f 9 45	262.0	.... Elko		f 5 27
f 9 52	265.5	.... Crookton		f 5 18
f 10 00	269.5	.... Doyle		f 5 09
....	270.4	.... Bonita		....
10 16	276.8	.... Parlin		4 52
f 10 28	282.2	.... Mounds		f 4 40
f 10 45	288.6	ar .... Gunnison lv		4 25
f 10 50	288.6	lv .... Gunnison .... ar		+ 4 20
11 02	294.5	.... Hierro		f 4 00
11 14	299.2	.... Iola		f 3 47
f 11 16	300.1	.... Kezar		f 3 45
f 11 36	307.2	.... Cebolla		f 3 25
f 11 54	314.1	.... Sapinero		3 05
....	315.1	.... Lake Junction		....
f 12 14	320.9	.... Curecanti		f 2 40
....	327.5	.... Crystal Creek		....
+ 12 40	329.0	ar .... Cimarron lv		2 15
1 00	329.0	lv .... Cimarron .... ar		**1 55**
1 35	334.6	.... Cerro Summit		**1 35**
1 58	341.3	.... Cedar Creek		**12 55**
f 2 10	346.4	.... Fairview		f 12 34
2 30	351.5	ar .... Montrose lv		**12 20**
2 45	351.5	lv .... Montrose .... ar		+ 12 01
f 3 01	357.4	.... Menoken		f 11 40
3 14	362.2	.... Olathe		11 26
f 3 27	367.5	.... Chipeta		f 11 10
3 45	372.8	.... Delta		10 56
f 3 55	377.5	.... Roubideau		f 10 34
f 4 02	380.2	.... Stratter		f 10 26
f 4 13	384.8	.... Escalente		f 10 14
f 4 28	390.9	.... Dominguez		f 9 55
f 4 45	397.7	.... Bridgeport		f 9 37
f 4 57	402.9	.... Deer Run		f 9 23
f 5 10	407.9	.... Kahnah		f 9 10
5 20	411.8	.... Whitewater		9 01
f 5 35	417.3	.... Unaweep		f 8 47
6 00	424.2	ar .... Grand Junction lv		8 30

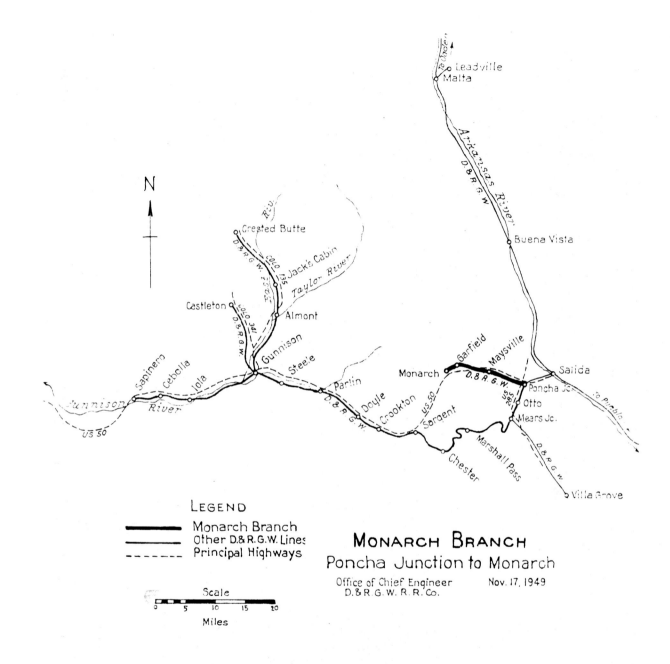

LEGEND

━━━━ Monarch Branch
──── Other D.&R.G.W. Lines
- - - - Principal Highways

MONARCH BRANCH
Poncha Junction to Monarch

Office of Chief Engineer   Nov. 17, 1949
D.&R.G.W.R.R.Co.

Scale
0   5   10   15   20
Miles

FOLLOWING PAGE. Engine #481, with heavy tonnage, descends the Monarch Branch. *John Krause, collection of Dr. Richard Severance*

MONARCH BRANCH
Narrow Gauge

BRIEF DESCRIPTION OF LINE FROM PHYSICAL AND CONSTRUCTION STANDPOINT

Built Poncha Junction to Maysville in 1881 and Maysville to Monarch in 1883. This line, 15.67 miles in length, reaches up the east side of the Continental Divide range and follows in general the highway route that crosses Monarch Pass. Terrain is rough with heavy grades with a maximum grade of 4.5 percent. Curvature is heavy with a number of 24 degree curves and one switchback.

Rail in place is approximately as follows:

Weight of Rail	Length	Date Laid
65#	9 miles	1929
85#	4 "	1929
90#	3 "	1946

This line is without special ballast other than natural gravel and fine rock developed in cuts during the construction.

ESTIMATED INVESTMENT COST TO DECEMBER 31, 1947
Val. Sec. Colo. 9-B   276,373.60

NORMAL MAINTENANCE ORGANIZATION

Section	-1 foreman with gang of 1 man during Winter and up to 3 men during Summer.
B&B	-1 gang, foreman and 6 men, covers territory Salida to Sapinero and portion of line between Mears Junction and Alamosa, Monarch, Crested Butte and Baldwin branches.
Water Service	-1 pipefitter covers territory Salida to Sapinero and Mears Junction to Villa Grove, Monarch, Crested Butte and Baldwin branches.

PREVIOUS PAGE. From Maysville on the Monarch Branch, trains doubled into Monarch after climbing 1,700 feet in a little over eight miles, including a switchback. When snow got deep, operations were discontinued for several months while quarry workers using explosives loosened thousands of tons of limestone for the next season's operations of six-times-a-week trains. After standard gauging of the branch in 1954, the #483 was transferred by flatcar to Alamosa and is now used on the Durango & Silverton Narrow Gauge Railroad. Locomotive #489 is at Maysville wye on December 29, 1952.

THE DENVER AND RIO GRANDE WESTERN RAILROAD COMPANY
Statement of Revenues, Expenses and Net Earnings
Monarch Branch - Years 1941 and 1948

SYSTEM REVENUES

	1941	1948
Freight Forwarded	$ 281,509	$ 550,251
Freight Received	1,065	5,660
Total System Revenues	$ 282,574	$555,911

BRANCH LINE

* Revenues	1941	1948
Freight Forwarded	$ 70,377	$ 137,574
Freight Received	266	1,434
Paid R.G.M. Way	—	Dr 79
Total Revenues	$ 70,643	$ 138,929
Expenses		
Maintenance of Way and Structures	$ 8,382	$ 20,365
Maintenance of Equipment	12,428	35,721
Transportation Expenses	28,093	87,388
Total Expenses	$ 48,903	$ 143,474
Net Operating Revenue	$ 21,740	D $ 4,545

* - Freight revenues Based on Revenue Ton Mile Prorate with Minimum 25%.
D- Donotes Deficit

BALANCE OF RAILROAD

	Basis I Expenses Computed on 50% Operating Ratio		Basis II "Out-of-Pocket" Expenses	Basis III "Full Operating" Expenses
	Year		Year	Year
	1941	1948	1948	1948
Revenues	$211,931	$ 416,982	$ 416,982	$416,982
Expenses	105,965	208,491	364,123	449,466
Net Operating Revenue	$105,966	$ 208,491	$ 52,859	D $ 32,484

TOTAL EARNINGS VALUE TO SYSTEM

Total System Net Earnings Unadjusted	$127,706	$ 203,946	$ 48,314	D $ 37,029
Adjusted Total System Net Earnings (1)	--	$ 203,946	$ 24,259	D $ 76,138
Estimated Total System Net Earnings After Allowing for Adjustment and Taxes	--	$ 195,320	$ 15,633	D $ 84,764

D- Denotes Deficit.
(1) Adjusted to allow for increased freight rates and wage rates—1949 over 1948.

Capital Expenditures	1941	1948
Road - Gross	$ 2,647	Cr $ 1,516
Road - Net	$ 2,647	Cr $ 498

Taxes

Ad Valorem	$ 6,764	$ 8,626

Statistics of Train Operation

	1941	1948
Number of Trains Operated	578	959
Train Miles	11,560	19,180
Gross Ton Miles (1000)	11,157	18,168
Net Ton Miles (1000)	6,204	10,005
Average Net Tons per Train	536	522
Average Net Tons per Day (306 Days per Year)	1,102	1,636

Basis I- Based on formula used in abandonment proceedings before the ICC.

Basis II- Based on out-of-pocket expenses, i.e., those that tend to vary with the train miles and car miles operated, including locomotive repairs, car rental (inc. repairs), fuel, trainmen and enginemen wages, water-lubricants-supplies for locomotives, enginehouse expense, transfer cost, and switching.

Basis III- Based on a gross ton mile proportion of full operating costs for M of W&S, M of E, and Transportation, as shown in the Income Account, excluding deferred Maintenance Credits.

Note: Year 1941 expenses not computed under Basis II and Basis III account necessary traffic flow data not available.

Budget and Statistics,
December 2, 1949

THE DENVER AND RIO GRANDE WESTERN RAILROAD COMPANY

Poncha Junction-Monarch Branch Station Earnings Freight and Passenger
Years 1934 to 1948, Inclusive

Year	Amount	Year	Amount	Year	Amount
1934	$ 113,930	1939	$ 199,128	1944	$ 253,033
1935	194,509	1940	270,201	1945	169,000
1936	132,959	1941	282,574	1946	255,483
1937	227,878	1942	356,431	1947	295,086
1938	86,985	1943	398,036	1948	555,911

	1941				1948			
	Freight For'd	Freight Rec'd	Passgr For'd	Total	Freight For'd	Freight Rec'd	Passgr For'd	Total
Garfield	$	$ 3	$	3	$	$ 15	$	15
Leonard	5			5				
Monarch	281,504	1,062		282,566	550,251	5,645		555,896
Total	$281,509	$1,065		$282,574	$550,251	$ 5,660		$555,911

Branch Line
Proportion-
Minimum 25%

	Freight For'd	Freight Rec'd		Total	Freight For'd	Freight Rec'd		Total
	$70,377	$ 266		$70,643	$137,574	$ 1,434		$139,008
Paid RGMW				—				79
				$70,643				$138,929

Mail	—	—
Express	—	—
Miscellaneous	—	—
Total Branch Line	$70,643	$138,929

Freight Accounting Department,
June 22, 1949

THE DENVER AND RIO GRANDE WESTERN RAILROAD COMPANY

Commodities Handled On Poncha Junction-Monarch Branch.
Years 1941 and 1948

Commodities	1941 Cars	1941 Tons	1941 (System Revenue)	1948 Cars	1948 Tons	1948 (System Revenue)
Local Freight Originated At and Destined to Points on the Branch						
NONE						
Freight Moved From Branch Points To System Points And To Branch Points From System Points						
Product of Mines, NOS	1	13	$ 45			
Bituminous Coal	5	119	428	6	136	$ 573
Gravel and Sand				1	17	80
Ties, Railroad				2	14	47
Explosives, NOS	5	48	445	3	43	535
All LCL Freight		7	82		32	649
Total	11	187	$ 1,000	12	242	$ 1,884
Freight Moved From Branch Points to Points on Other Roads And to Branch Points From Other Roads						
Fluxing Stone & Raw Dolomite	5,650	305,761	$281,300	9,472	489,645	$549,749
Machinery and Machines, NOS				5	163	3,677
Explosives, NOS				1	12	159
Scrap Iron & Steel	1	30	135	1	36	240
All LCL Freight		8	139		7	202
Total	5,651	305,799	$281,574	9,479	489,863	$554,027
Grand Total	5,662	305,986	$282,574	9,491	490,105	$555,911

Freight Accounting Department.
June 22, 1949

Engine #489 drops down on December 29, 1952 to the lower portion of the switchback with 13 cars of limestone. It will come back up and take down the remaining portion of its 26-car train and the caboose. Coupled up, the two portions then will drop down to Maysville, and the engine and caboose will return to Monarch to bring down another 26 loads, so that the train into Salida is of the usual 52 cars of limestone. One time while the crew was taking the first 13 cars down the switchback, the rear half of the train ran away, through the switch and piled up on the granite rock wall at the tail of the switchback.

This train with a Helper on the rear works on the 4% grade between the Monarch switchback and the quarry. *Clayton Tanner*

Locomotive #483 is the Helper on a 26-car cut of empties heading up the Monarch Branch, having just rounded the half-circle curve where it crossed U.S. 50 a mile or so west of Maysville.

The #483 works up the Monarch Branch in 1955 at the head of a 52-car train of empties, with a Helper engine at the rear. Near this point at the old townsite of Maysville, the train will be reduced and doubled to Monarch.

The #489 has brought down the first half of its train to the upper switch of the Monarch Branch switchback. It will spot these at the lower switch then come back up to bring down the second half and the caboose. The track at this upper stub held only an engine and 15 cars. One time while the engine was down at the lower switch, the second portion of the train ran away and crashed into the rocky end of the spur, destroying several cars.

Workers are standard gauging the Monarch Branch in 1956 at the highway crossing about a mile before the end of the track. The huge pile of waste required relocation of the track.

Standard gauging the Monarch Branch in 1956. This is the scene at the lower switch of the switchback.

This is one of the sharp curves on the Monarch Branch during conversion to standard gauge. A test track was used at Denver to determine if the diesels to be used would be able to negotiate the curves.

Engine #481 drifts past the closed Poncha Junction station with a train of limestone from the Monarch Branch. A telegraph operator was stationed here through the busy World War II years to handle the traffic from Monarch and Crested Butte. *Clayton Tanner*

Engine #485 backs half a train of empties, 13 cars, up the switchback on the Monarch Branch. After it has cleared the upper switch, it will wait for the rear end Helper to bring the second half of the train up the switchback. Coupled up, the 26-car train and caboose will go onto Monarch. The tail of the switchback would accommodate about 15 cars and an engine. *Clayton Tanner*

OPPOSITE RIGHT. Locomotive #489 has taken one cut of loaded cars down the switchback and is entering the upper switch and will then back to the second cut of loads waiting above the switch. The tail track from the upper switch holds just an engine and about 15 cars.

The #481 approaches Monarch on August 3, 1951 at the head of a long train of 52 empty gondolas. The grade here was 4%.

Locomotive #483 arrives at Monarch in 1955. The 26-car train would have a Helper engine working back by the caboose, as the grade here was 4%. The track at this point had to be moved occasionally as the waste pile from the quarry encroached on the track. The train had climbed just under 3,000 feet in its 15-mile journey from Salida.

Locomotive #489 is on the tail of the Monarch wye. The original line had a gallows-type 50-foot turntable designed for small engines only. In the 1920s as the quarry came into full operation, a wye was built.

TOP RIGHT. The #489 has shoved one cut of cars up into the loading area at Monarch and now prepares to drop the caboose and spot the other half of its train. Barely seen are a number of car bodies for use by the carmen assigned here, including a coach and a former Western Union box car.

BOTTOM RIGHT. Having set out half their train at Maysville siding, the two engines start up on the stiff grades to the switchback. By this time Maysville had virtually disappeared as a community. It had a long siding and a wye.

OPPOSITE LEFT. At this point the track made a half circle crossing U.S. 50, for which the engine is blowing a warning whistle blast. Hidden from view are most of the train's 26 gondolas and the Helper engine located behind the caboose. The train would be split upon reaching the switchback.

THIRD DIVISION
THIRD DISTRICT
Mears Jct. and Alamosa

WESTWARD SECOND CLASS 323 Freight — Leave Tuesday Thurs. and Sat.	WESTWARD FIRST CLASS 317 Denver, Alamosa and Durango Passenger — Leave Daily Exc. Sunday	Distance from Denver	Time Table No. 100 March 28, 1920 — STATIONS	Distance from Alamosa	Siding Capacity in Cars — Passing Tracks	EASTWARD FIRST CLASS 318 Denver, Alamosa and Durango Passenger — Arrive Daily Exc. Sunday	EASTWARD SECOND CLASS 324 Freight — Arrive Mon, Wed and Friday
		215.11	S SALIDA N	85.33	Yard		3.31 PM
			10.9				
9.40 AM	4.50 PM	226.02	MEARS JUNC. RWCY	74.42	32	11.26 AM	3.01
			3.55				
10.20	f 5.15	229.57	PONCHA PASS Y	70.87	36	f 11.12	1.40
			3.26				
10.57 318	f 5.27	232.83	ROUND HILL WY	67.61	50	f 10.57 323	1.02
			6.16				
11.18	f 5.42	238.99	LINTON	61.45	46	f 10.41	12.41
			6.35				
11.43	s 5.57	245.34	Vg VILLA GROVE RDWCY	55.10	45	s 10.25	12.01 PM
			5.59				
12.15 PM	f 6.12	250.93	MINERAL HOT SPRINGS	49.51	49	f 10.09	11.36
			6.08				
12.50	f 6.27	257.01	MIRAGE	43.43	49	f 9.54	11.06
			5.68				
1.15 / 3.00	s 6.44	262.69	Mf MOFFAT DWY	37.75	103	s 9.40	10.33
			6.21				
3.25	f 7.00	268.90	LA GARITA	31.54	49	f 9.19	10.08
			5.40				
3.47	f 7.12	274.30	GIBSON	26.14	49	f 9.02	9.33
			5.97				
4.12	s 7.26	280.27	Gr HOOPER D	20.17	49	s 8.44	9.07
			6.57				
4.34	f 7.41	286.84	MOSCA	13.60	49	f 8.25	8.38
			7.27				
5.00	f 7.59	294.11	McGINTY	6.33	39	f 8.09	8.00 AM
			6.33				
5.45 PM	8.20 PM	300.44	As-Rm ALAMOSA RNWCYT		Yard	7.50 AM	
Arrive Tuesday Thurs. and Sat	Arrive Daily Exc. Sunday		(85.33)			Leave Daily Exc. Sunday	Leave Monday Wed. and Friday
(8.05)	(3.30)		........Time Over District.......			(3.36)	(7.31)
9.21	21.26		....Average Miles Per Hour....			20.67	9.90

C-1. EASTWARD TRAINS ARE SUPERIOR TO WESTWARD TRAINS OF THE SAME CLASS.

C-2. No train will leave Alamosa without clearance.

C-3. The west wye switch at Alamosa is set and locked for La Veta line. Third Division trains will come to full stop before entering Alamosa yard.

C-4. Passenger trains will not exceed a speed of fifteen miles per hour and freight trains ten miles per hour downgrade between Poncha Pass and Mears Junction and Poncha Pass and Round Hill.

C-5. Alder, at MP 236.9 is mail station for Nos. 317 and 318.

This is Mears Junction looking west. The trestle in the far distance carries the Valley Line which departed the main track at a switch beyond the telephone booth, using a half circle to start the climb to Poncha Pass. The two cars of rip-rap were for occasional washouts. The 18"x5' foot wooden sign was purchased by me, along with all the other wooden signs when the Gunnison lines were abandoned in 1954. Two-sided, bolted to a heavy post, the duplicate was auctioned at the 2003 National Narrow Gauge Convention for $1,400.

No. 85. Freight.	TELEGRAPH, WATER AND COALING STATIONS	TIME TABLE No. 12 Sept. 11th, 1881. STATIONS AND Passing Places		DISTANCES FROM DENVER	FIRST CLASS No. 91. Passenger.	No. 83. Passenger.
	NW	Dep	Denver	Dep	8 00 Am	7 30 Pm
6 00 Am	NWC	Dep	Salida	Dep 217.	7 30 Pm	9 05 Am
6 30	DW	"	Poncha	" 222.4	Ar 7 50 Pm	9 20
7 04		"	Toll Gate	" 225.7		9 42
7 28	D	"	Mears	" 228.		10 00
7 51	DC	"	Shirley	" 230.2		10 15
8 51		"	Gray's Siding	" 236.		10 55
9 59	D	"	Marshall Pass	" 242.6		11 41 AM
10 31		"	Siding No. 7	" 245.7		12 02 PM
11 04		"	Mill Switch	" 248.9		12 24
11 21 Am		"	Siding No. 9	" 250.6		12 36
12 05 Pm		"	Siding No. 10	" 254.9		1 05
12 35	DC	"	Aureo	" 259.2		1 20 Ar 1 40 Dep
1 31		"	Crooks	" 267.6		2 11
1 57		"	Doyle	" 271.5		2 25
2 55	D	"	Parlins	" 279.4		2 55
3 17		"	Cochotopa	" 282.4		3 07
4 15 PM	DWC	Ar	Gunnison	Ar 290.7		3 40 PM
(10.15)		(73.7)			(20)	(6.35)

RIGHT. Locomotive #482 heads the first "double" up Poncha Pass on February 14, 1951 from Mears Junction. Many gondolas were used by the dismantlers of the Valley Line which was being abandoned. The main line to Marshall Pass crosses under the trestle. The track at left connects (out of sight) with the main line, enabling engines coming off the Valley Line to be simply turned around by backing under the trestle. It was a compact, very simple track layout, a gem admired by many modelers.

A "double" starts the climb to Poncha Pass from Mears Junction. Four or five cars of coal was the tonnage limit on the steep 4% grade.

OPPOSITE RIGHT. On February 15, 1951 this train with #482 in the lead made the last trip on the Valley Line. It's shown here as it nears Round Hill at the approach to Poncha Pass.

Fall storms had barely dusted the Sangre de Cristos with snow as this train works its way north of Villa Grove heading for Poncha Pass. For the decade of the 1890s, this was a fairly busy branch handling the Denver-Durango passenger trains with their Pullmans, but after a new standard gauge line was opened to Alamosa over La Veta Pass, the importance of the branch dwindled.

OPPOSITE RIGHT TOP. Against a stormy background of the Sangre de Cristos, the monthly Valley Line train heads for Poncha Pass. The ruined hotel in the ghost town of Mineral Hot Springs is at right. This January 14, 1949 scene was photographed at the end of the 53-mile tangent on this little-used line.

OPPOSITE RIGHT BOTTOM. Against a background of the Sangre de Cristo Range, on November 4, 1949 a monthly freight heads for Alamosa after dropping down Poncha Pass. Ahead lies Villa Grove and beyond that the 53-mile tangent. The coal in the train is from the Baldwin Branch; the passenger cars are being deadheaded back to Alamosa after being used on an excursion out of Salida.

The Sangre de Cristo mountain range was an impressive backdrop for the infrequent trains on the Valley Line, Alamosa to Mears Junction. This train with Engine #480 and 13 cars works on the 16-mile grade in November of 1950 from Villa Grove, finally crossing Poncha Pass at 9,059 feet, having climbed 1,100 feet. This very dry valley seldom received much snow, but Poncha Pass often required a flanger plow train to open it for the monthly train.

Doubling Poncha Pass, the last Salida-Alamosa run on February 14, 1951 is centered in the camera lens, with #482 in the lead and #480 at the rear at Mears Junction. Behind it is caboose #0589 and the end of an era. *Robert W. Richardson, collection of Mallory Hope Ferrell*

Engine #481 drags an extra tender, used as an idler car, five standard gauge refrigerator cars, and #268 near Hooper on the Valley Line in December of 1950. The #268 had been in storage following the 1949 Chicago Railroad Fair; it is destined for Salida to be used on the branch lines surrounding the Gunnison area. *Robert W. Richardson, collection of Mallory Hope Ferrell*

LEFT. Behind me is my pickup truck off the road at a 45 degree angle at Poncha Pass on January 28, 1949. To prepare to take this picture on the Poncha Pass road, I had driven off onto what I thought was the berm, but it turned out to be just snow pushed there by highway crews. I learned the hard way not to expect anything solid at the edge of the roads in Colorado. The crews, of course, stared at my predicament as they went by, and later commented to me they'd expected something like this to happen. They were greatly surprised to see me waiting for them at the crossing on the other side of the pass. A friendly rancher with a five-ton truck stopped, and with his chain and mine, I was back on the road in minutes!

BOTTOM LEFT. Coming down the south side of Poncha Pass, the two engines of a Mears Junction to Poncha Pass turn have left all except the flanger and caboose and are plowing open the line. Only a mile further the snow was barely over the top of the rails. They passed up Round Hill tank and wye as the snow was still badly drifted there and went on to Villa Grove, another 13 miles, where they could take water and wye without problems. Locomotives #499 and #496 are tailed by #0586 on January 28, 1949.

BOTTOM RIGHT. How cold weather and poor track conditions affected operations is illustrated by this train. Class K-37 Mikados #499 and #496 with a flanger car behind the first engine and seven cars of coal work up the 4% grade from Mears Junction to Poncha Pass. There hadn't been a train on this track for about a month, and although the combined rating of the two engines was 504 tons under the best of conditions, they are actually moving a net tonnage of about 375 tons. The dispatcher and the conductor made allowances for the rusty rail, occasional drifts and low temperature, so they doubled their train on this steep three miles on January 28, 1949.

LEFT. Not working hard at all, #499 and #496 drop down the south side of Poncha Pass, plowing open the drifts that had accumulated. The crew left their train at the pass, while they ran to Villa Grove with just the flanger and caboose. There they wyed and returned to the top of the pass, the #496 taking the train alone onto Alamosa on January 28, 1949. The snow was dry and fluffy and blew around a great deal, and soon the same cuts were full again.

BELOW LEFT. Villa Grove's unique little tank could just handle two engines nicely as #499, #496 and caboose #0586 depart on January 28, 1949. It would be lunchtime for the crew before they could wye and return to Poncha Pass. A snowstorm was in progress on the northern peaks of the Sangre de Cristo Range.

OPPOSITE. Conductor Young hands up orders for the last run on the Valley Line at Alamosa on February 15, 1951. Except for the 20 miles of dual gauge from Alamosa to Hooper, the line to Mears Junction was abandoned. A holdover from times when much smaller engines were used, the idler car is an old engine tender, but today it is hauled empty. The standard gauge cars will be set out for loading at Mosca and Hooper. The two box cars and caboose will go on through to Salida. Engine #482 was returned to Alamosa on a standard gauge flat car within several years for use during the "pipe rush."

MEARS JUNCTION TO ALAMOSA

73.44 MILES

Rise 682' Fall 1567'

Built N.G. from Mears Jct. to Villa Grove in 1881, to Alamosa in 1890.
" S.G. " Hooper to Alamosa in 1930.

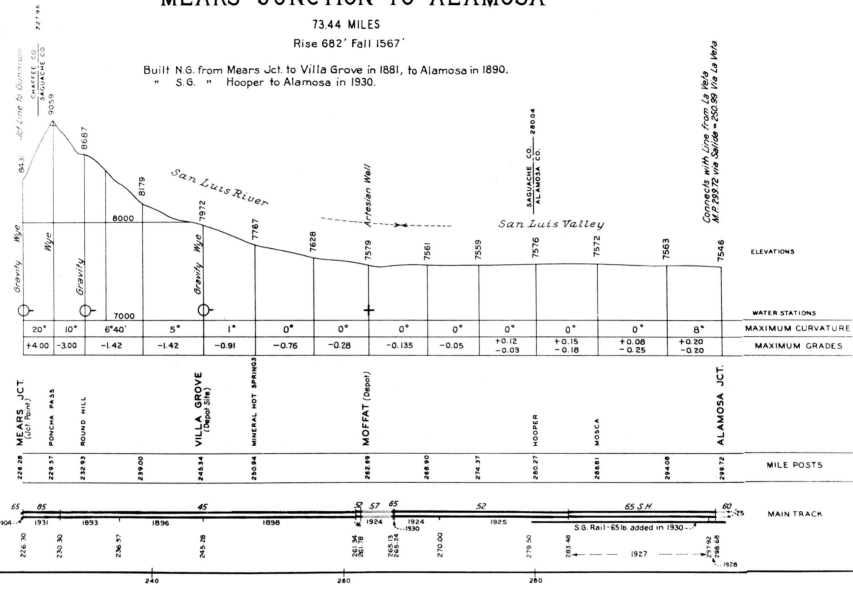

20°	10°	6°40'	5°	1°	0°	0°	0°	0°	0°	0°	0°	8°		MAXIMUM CURVATURE
+4.00	-3.00	-1.42	-1.42	-0.91	-0.76	-0.28	-0.135	-0.05	+0.12 / -0.03	+0.15 / -0.18	+0.08 / -0.25	+0.20 / -0.20		MAXIMUM GRADES

152

ABOVE. Strung out on the hillside between Poncha Junction and Mears Junction is the last train destined to make the final run from Mears to Alamosa on February 14, 1951. Locomotives #482 and #480 took the empties to the summit of Poncha Pass, then #480 returned light to Salida, while #482 took empty gondolas to sidings for use by the dismantlers who soon commenced taking up the track starting at Hooper and working north.

The last C-16 Class #268 brings a short train of empties out of Crested Butte on July 3, 1952. As no other engines were stationed at Gunnison, #268 handled all branch line work from that point. The mountains are topped with snow in this mid-summer scene.

Five

THE THIRD DIVISION:
GUNNISON TO OURAY

Little attention has been paid to the Crested Butte Branch, even though it provided a great amount of coal traffic that kept the lines into the Gunnison area going. When the last big coal mine at Crested Butte closed in 1952, abandonment of those lines soon followed.

For most of its 29 miles, the branch was in open ranch country following the Slate River on an easy grade on which a single K-36 or K-37 could move a long train of empty gondolas. The town was at an elevation of 8,878 feet, only 1,200 feet higher than Gunnison. The trademark mountain loomed over it from the east. There were tremendous coal deposits in the area, and various abandoned workings could be noted on the mountain slopes.

Gradually these mines closed until only the "Big Mine" located on the tail of the wye was in operation, supplying the steel plant at Pueblo with most of its coking coal. At some places in the mountain, anthracite was encountered, but the demand dropped to where but one car of it was shipped for about every 100 cars of the bituminous.

The yard was fairly large in comparison with other D&RGW yards, reflecting busier times when a switch engine was used at Crested Butte. Until the advent of the Rio Grande Motorway and its planned replacement of branch trains, a daily mixed had been operated. Many years ago the train had one of the cupola-equipped baggage-coach cars.

In 1893 just when the famed financial crash hit Colorado and the nation, the D&RG completed the Ruby Anthracite Branch from Crested Butte. It is better known as the Floresta Branch from the anthracite mine at its terminus. Just a little more than 11 miles long, it climbed 1,000 feet, and its final several miles featured a region plagued by snow and avalanches. This was so bad the line would close in November and reopen in spring using a rotary. In the recession following World War I, the mine closed and never reopened, but it was years before the track was removed.

About the only use for the rotary stationed at Gunnison was to reopen the upper end of the Crested Butte Branch which some winters would get very deep snow, beyond the capacity of a flanger train. In January of 1952 in the snowiest winter for some 35 years, the rotary made its final trip. In June of that year the Big Mine closed on account of a steel strike, and the next month Colorado Fuel & Iron announced it would not reopen as it had developed a new source of coal on their Colorado & Wyoming Ry. in southern Colorado.

Whatever engines were available at Gunnison were used on the branch, as even the smaller C-16s could bring a good-sized train of loads down. The two former Crystal River engines were frequently used, but #360 went to scrap in 1950, and #361 followed a year later due to damage incurred when it was trapped in a slush slide along the Slate Cut area of the branch.

At that point the valley narrowed for a mile or so, and the flanger train apparently triggered the slide which froze, and the engine itself was frozen before it could be dug out.

Gunnison was the last place to use the two remaining C-16s, #268 and #278, and they were employed on infrequent runs on the Baldwin and Sapinero branches and even on trips to Crested Butte. A single K-36 or K-37 handled the coal trains east, with two or even three Helpers over Marshall Pass.

Crested Butte, with the end of coal activity, declined in population, and then came the skiers, and now it's a popular ski resort area, with stores reopened and houses rebuilt and year-around population almost back to where it was during coal mining times. The depot became the public library and was early-on recipient of a sizable gift of cash with instructions to buy railroad books! The highway west to Kebler Pass is largely located on the former grade of the Floresta Branch.

To Gunnison to See the Last C-16 Do a Winter Turn

The dispatcher's "dope sheet," outlining the branch runs in days to come, had a surprise, a trip on the Sapinero Branch, a now rare event. So I was up that spring morning of March 11, 1952 at 4:30 to head out on the three-hour trip to Gunnison. The roads were empty, and I met one vehicle in the entire distance, and understandably, there wasn't a single place to get a cup of coffee.

My trip was slowed a bit by Colorado's freak highway conditions. Ascending Monarch Pass, I found the night plows had left just a skiff of snow on the road, but the rising sun briefly melted the top of that skiff, which just as

Engine #268 near Almont makes a caboose hop on July 3, 1952 to Crested Butte to bring some empty gondolas to Gunnison after doing routine switching needed at that point. It was the last C-16 on the D&RGW, and the only locomotive stationed at Gunnison.

The C-16 #268 is on the Big Mine track at Crested Butte on July 3, 1952. The loading dock of the mine is in the distant left, and part of town is at right. The mine had permanently shut down, and #268 was sent to bring in some empty gondolas to Gunnison where they were included in a freight for Salida. The cars were needed at Alamosa for the "pipe rush" loadings.

quickly froze, giving the road a thin, slippery coating. My Chevy pickup, I found, would advance over this at about 22 mph, but if I tried pushing it a little more, it would spin out. And that's what, without planning, I did, finding the truck spun around and headed downhill!

My only solution was to drive down a mile or so where some loose rock outcropping was next to the berm. After some 300 pounds of that was loaded into the bed, I had no more difficulty reaching the 11,000 ft. summit. It's just one of those little things that happens when taking photographs in winter in Colorado!

I passed the Monarch switchback and quarry on the way up, with the tracks deeply snow-covered and no sign of trains for several months. Soon the quarry workers would have their elaborate charges completed, and in one blast, bring down many thousands of tons of limestone, and then the railroad would be busy for another nine months.

There were several box cars of lumber waiting at Sapinero by a little sawmill that stubbornly insisted on railroad service, disdaining the offers of Rio Grande Motorway. Truckloads of lumber often arrived at their destination in not very pretty condition, with the ends, wet or frozen, and quite dirty from splashing water from the highway.

At 8 a.m. I checked the roundhouse and the #268, last of the small engines, was sitting next to the turntable getting up steam, so there was time to hit the only open restaurant in town. Its other customers were several rancher types who didn't help my appetite by wolfing down very raw hamburger steaks which appeared to be just browned on the top and bottom.

Finishing oiling around, Engineer Clayt Braswell eased his yellow charge onto the table and the work day began in earnest. Next there was a stop to get coal from the dock, then a stop at the water tank, and then the short train was made up. The narrow gauge's sole wedgeplow was eased from its spur, and then a drag flanger and two cabooses were coupled on.

We were ready for the 26 miles of mostly Gunnison Canyon, where the experienced crew knew they'd find cuts full of snow and in some places, lengthy drifts. The #268 had bucked those miles many a time

In the winter of 1951-52 Crested Butte received more snow than at any time in more than 30 years. The rotary snowplow from Gunnison was needed to open the rail line and clear the yard tracks. The snow banks were so high at street intersections that motorists tied rags to the top of car antennas. In this March 29, 1952 view the station and its outbuildings in the distance appear to be half hidden by snow. Although more snow fell, no further use was made of the rotary.

The Crested Butte Branch from Gunnison experienced heavy snowfall, especially on the last 12 miles into Crested Butte. When engines with plow pilots or a flanger car could not push the snow away, the rotary snowplow, kept at Gunnison, made a trip. Engine #486 finds little snow on the track near Jack's Cabin after a rotary trip on March 29, 1952. The snow banks are the remains of the rotary's trip.

since 1882. Wedgeplow #09271 was a veteran of Black Canyon episodes galore, a place where rotaries didn't dare venture because of rocks, and slides with not only rocks, but trees, as well. The road's "littlest" caboose, #0524, housed the sectionmen, with their shovels (and picks, too), with the larger #0588 following.

The train was sort of symbolic of how things had changed. The engine had looked lost in that otherwise empty roundhouse, where so many locomotives of all classes used to be seen. The usual line of silent engines was long gone from the yard. The once very busy car repair yard was empty, with no one around.

There wasn't much snow at Gunnison; it was barely up to the top of the rails. But the crews studied the Western skies where a mass of dark clouds were gathering. Somewhere out beyond the entrance to Black Canyon a storm was having its way, and its way was headed for the Gunnison country. Everyone had packed heavy lunches plus, the best preparation that could be made for what might be a long trip, one that might test the 16-hour work limit.

At a 12- to 15-mph pace the train headed west. The first couple of miles were in fairly straight and open country, then occasionally an odd drift was encountered. Then the train crossed the river and wound through the narrow ledge behind trees that lined the stream.

From the highway across the river I got glimpses of the train, but no photographs could mark its progress. Then a few miles out, it rounded a curve cautiously, for there ahead was a long stretch of track that was deep in snow, some of it higher than the engine's stack. Just beyond was the highway crossing of a side road, which certainly helped me in my picture pursuit. Stopping short, Braswell properly blew the whistle signal for flagging, though no engine was nearer than Salida.

The sectionmen trudged alongside the engine and commenced shoveling a few feet of rail to give the engine a footing. Then with flanger and cabooses uncoupled, the little engine, with a roar, pushed the rock-laden plow with its big engine-style plow into the snow.

The first attack gained somewhat less than a hundred feet. Then it backed up to the starting point and waited while the laborers shoveled clear rails as far as they could. This location was going to require several runs, as this wasn't the usual wintertime powdery fluffy stuff; this was layers of various snowfalls, packed down layer by layer with a crust of hard stuff, like layers of a cake.

With drivers spinning, the #268 pushed the heavy plow as fast as Braswell dared, and it carried through the snow until the banks at the side of the cab were higher than the cab. Once more the engine backed away.

But now there was a diversion—the sectionmen, instead of going forward to clear rails—were in a group busily shoveling at something beside the track, and then they reached down and up came the Gunnison foreman, covered with snow.

The sectionman knew where to walk, but he didn't know of a culvert at that point, and he'd gone down with several feet of snow over his

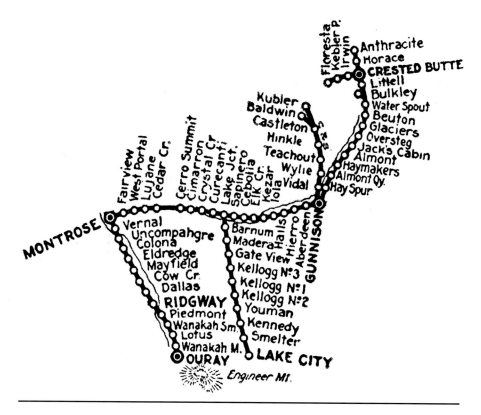

THIRD DIVISION
CRESTED BUTTE BRANCH
Gunnison and Anthracite

WESTWARD				EASTWARD	
SECOND CLASS			Siding Capacity in Cars	SECOND CLASS	
347 Crested Butte Mixed Leave Daily	Distance from Denver	Time Table No. 100 March 28, 1920 STATIONS	Distance from Anthracite	Passing Tracks	348 Denver Mixed Arrive Daily
10.35 AM	288.64	Gu GUNNISON RNWCYT	31.95	Yard	4.00 PM
		10.85			
f 11.10	299.49	ALMONT	21.10	45	f 2.55
		5.23			
f 11.40	304.72	JACK'S CABIN W	15.87	27	f 2.30
		5.78			
f 12.10 PM	310.50	GLACIERS	10.09		f 2.07
		5.79			
12.45 PM	316.29	Be CRESTED BUTTE RDWCY	4.30	Yard	1.50 PM
		0.70			
	316.99	FLORESTA JUNCTION	3.60		
		3.60			
	320.59	ANTHRACITE		39	
Arrive Daily		(31.95)			Leave Daily
(2.10) 14.74		........Time Over District....... ....Average Miles Per Hour....			(2.10) 14.74

I-1. EASTWARD TRAINS ARE SUPERIOR TO WESTWARD TRAINS OF THE SAME CLASS.
I-2. No train will leave Gunnison or Crested Butte without clearance.
I-3. No. 348 will wait at Crested Butte until No. 347 arrives.

159

head. It didn't help that he was on the short side as to stature. His temper and patience was to be sorely tried the rest of the day as various crew members waxed sarcastic in asides such as admonishing him that this was no time to go playing in the snow, etc.

The third try was successful and the engine reached the road crossing, then it backed to get its train while the sectionmen picked open the crossing (this was no time to have a derailment). They coupled up the outfit, and it was on its way again at a cautious 12 mph perhaps, now and then encountering a drift, and from way across the valley where it opened out at Iola, I could tell by the tall columns of smoke that those drifts were frequent.

The canyon then closed in, and the road climbed higher, and the train vanished into the deep canyon. I could only drive on to Cebolla, seven miles farther where both the railroad and highway shared the narrow space on the north side of the river.

It was a long wait, a couple hours it seemed, and the storm's advance portion was in full force as the train appeared, with the plow coated with snow up to the headlight mounted on a little tower just behind it. With the wind blowing and snow in big flakes making picture taking iffy, I managed at least one desirable shot as the train passed.

In the seven miles yet to go, there was little opportunity for photos, and the train was obscured mostly by rocks, brush, its own smoke and the storm. Then rounding into Sapinero Needles' big curve, there was a break in the storm. Ahead, after an open stretch of track with little snow, was a deep rock cut filled to the top, much above the engine's stack. There was a pause while steam built up, and the crew discussed the situation.

Meanwhile, I desperately sought a spot to pull off the pavement but the berm was deep in spring mud, and I didn't dare try to park it there. I couldn't park on the pavement either, however briefly, as there were too many locals who had their foot to the floor.

Driving very slowly, I watched the #268 take a run for the cut, the little drivers turning faster than I'd ever seen them, 25 mph or even more. As the plow hit the filled cut, I sort of involuntarily prayed there'd be no big rocks down there. Snow literally exploded high in the air, as I could imagine the caboose's occupants hanging firmly onto anything handy. The engine slowed abruptly, and yet kept working hard, but it looked like it might stall, and then very slowly it broke through—and kept going.

Beyond the countryside it was more open, and winds had scoured most of the snow from the track and right-of-way. In fact, when they wyed the plow at Sapinero, snow hardly covered the rails of the stub switch at the tail. Nine hours to cover 26 miles! A symbol of long ago was the last harp switchstand remaining on the Gunnison lines. Its target was bent by all those long-gone trainmen who had struggled with it for decades.

A gap in the storm happened just upon arrival at Sapinero, for a few minutes it was clear air. Then with a blast the main part of the storm hit,

BELOW. Locomotive #486 works hard to reopen the track to the Big Mine. The results of using the flanger car are obvious in the foreground. This was snow country, and now it's a popular ski resort. Up the valley in the background was the former Floresta Branch, which closed each winter and was reopened each spring with a rotary.

Out of sight in the snow are the remains of numerous coal mines which for decades kept the Crested Butte branch busy. As late as 1948 nearly 1,400 cars of coal made up the traffic.

On December 3, 1952, #483 passes near the small community of Almont on a caboose hop to Crested Butte.

The winter snows were still not too deep for Engine #483 without a plow pilot to work the Crested Butte yard. But after this December 3, 1952 scene, much more snow was to accumulate. A storm was descending on the town as this scene was taken.

With its flanger car and plow pilot, Engine #486 has been clearing Crested Butte trackage. The snow in town was piled as high as the theater marquee.

Spring is nowhere in sight in this mountain scene. Class K-36 #486 switches gondolas of coal at Crested Butte on a cold March 29, 1952 in knee-deep snow. The #486 was retired from the D&RGW in 1962 and displayed at the Royal Gorge Park, but years later retrieved by the Durango & Silverton in exchange for #499. *Robert W. Richardson, collection of Mallory Hope Ferrell*

Blowing off a little extra steam over the holidays, #268 crosses the East River bridge on the Crested Butte Branch on July 3, 1952. The Crested Butte and Baldwin branches were abandoned in 1955. *Robert W. Richardson, collection of Mallory Hope Ferrell*

CRESTED BUTTE BRANCH

28.24 MILES

Rise 1206' Fall 3'
Built N.G. to Crested Butte in 1881.
" " " Anthracite in 1882.
Track Removed Crested Butte to Anthracite in 1947

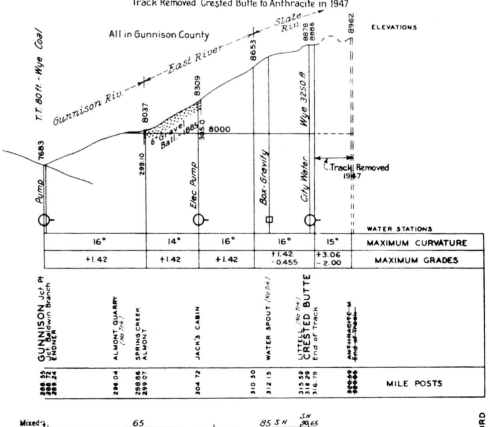

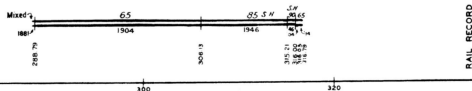

Locomotive #278 and caboose #0588 run light on July 7, 1949 to Sapinero to pick up loads of scrap from the abandoned Black Canyon line. The C-16 dated to 1882, a product of Baldwin. It was given to Montrose in 1952 and is now on display at a bridge over the Cimarron River at Cimarron, Colorado. The caboose was given to Lake City for display and was trucked there without the Gunnison crew having a chance to get their work clothes, etc., so they drove to Lake City, retrieved their items and then filed a pay claim as if they had made a train trip. Management paid.

boiling black clouds above barely visible through heavy large flakes of snow.

The little yard and the train vanished from sight, and I reluctantly realized the day was about over, certainly as far as photos were concerned, and that I best head back to Alamosa. The calendar might indicate it was spring, but the weather sure didn't.

Most of the way home was in a heavy snowfall. Ascending 11,312-foot Monarch Pass I could see little of the road ahead, and suddenly there in my lane was a boulder as high as the hood, which I missed by a sudden swerve. I couldn't warn the Highway Department, as everything at the summit was dark and closed, but at Poncha Springs I found a phone at last. Once over Poncha Pass the San Luis Valley stretched 100 miles with just traces of the storm reaching it.

Today the #268 sits on display in Pioneer Park in Gunnison. It still sports the "Grande Gold" paint scheme it wore in its final operational years, a sort of heritage of its visit to the Chicago Railroad Fair in 1949. Its bell was stolen while in the roundhouse, but it still can be heard if you attend a certain luncheon club's meetings.

Like most county historical societies, the Gunnison museum was oriented to genealogy and ancestor history with one exception. The widow of a railroader took care that railroad exhibits were set up and maintained indoors. They were relics of when Gunnison was headquarters of the Third Division, when that was the main line until 1890, and later as headquarters of the successor Gunnison Division. It was a fitting home for the last operating C-16.

Through the Black Canyon

In October of 1945 I was just out of the Army and took a month's trip to Colorado. At the Denver office, Perlman had not yet become a power, and they readily issued me a permit to ride narrow gauge freight trains, provided I had purchased a ticket in advance, as conductors were not permitted to accept cash fares.

Ticket clerks had to hunt for the tariffs, but they eventually supplied me with roundtrips for the Baldwin and Crested Butte branches, and a one-way ticket from Gunnison to Montrose. The fares were mostly two cents a mile, with a reduction for roundtrips.

Engine #361 switches at Cimarron on September 19, 1948. The C-21 had delivered a Rocky Mountain Railroad Club excursion from Gunnison that day. *Robert W. Richardson, collection of Mallory Hope Ferrell*

D&RGW #360 on the hill east of the Cimmaron depot switches a string of gondolas, part of a scrap train that was pulling up rails from Cerro Summit. Note the old automobiles in this July 7, 1949 scene. *Robert W. Richardson, collection of Mallory Hope Ferrell*

Former Crystal River R.R. #101, the #360, turns on the wye at Sapinero at the mouth of the Black Canyon to replace its fellow Class C-21 #361 which had broken down and was stranded with an excursion train on September 19, 1948. The three ex-CR engines were the only outside-frame 2-8-0 types on the D&RGW narrow gauge.

Locomotive #360 is being used by the contractor dismantling the old narrow gauge main line from Sapinero to Cedar Creek on July 7, 1949. At left is the Cimarron tank, and hardly noticeable in the foreground is the little Cimarron River, whose narrow canyon to the right was used to enter the Black Canyon.

On September 24, 1951 Engine #278 works hard east of Sapinero. Tonnage was so close to the engine's maximum that it dropped down to about five miles per hour. At the right of this scene is parked the Chevy "g-buster" carryall used for years by the Abandoned Lines Reporter.

I learned when an infrequent freight would be leaving Gunnison, and that morning found me waiting hours because of various delays. Finally, in late morning, we headed west with about 15 cars. The scenery changed from the open valley of Gunnison to a winding, ever-deeper canyon of the river, sort of a prelude to the Black Canyon itself, 26 miles further. Our stops in the Gunnison Canyon were only for water and some switching at Sapinero.

Power was one of the "little Mudhens," as some railroaders called them, the two Class C-21 outside-frame 2-8-0s purchased from the Crystal River Railroad in 1916. The crew informed me they were the heaviest engines permitted west of Sapinero, as bridge clearances were dangerously close for a K-27 Class Mudhen and so were not worked through.

Although it was a bright, sunny fall day, I soon learned why it was named "Black." The bright sun only intensified the dark shadows of the deep canyon whose walls in places were near 2,000 feet above the river.

With the crew's permission, I sat atop the cupola, the conductor remarking "the permit doesn't say you can't" and smiled. The scenery was impressive even though there were few opportunities for good pictures on account of those deep shadows. Way up on the canyon walls was what appeared to be loose boulders the size of an apartment house, and they looked ready to come down any moment.

There was only one siding at Curecanti, near the strange-pointed rock that rose high on the south side of the river, and which was used in the railroad's emblem for more than 50 years, the Curecanti Needle.

Eventually we came along the north bank, gradually gaining some altitude. At a place called Crystal Creek, we crossed a steel trestle and the husky engine ahead really began to work hard. It was only two miles up this narrow side canyon to Cimarron, but the wind was strong, and I arrived at Cimarron coated with cinders, tear-streaked from flicking some out of my eyes.

Cimarron, now a part of the National Park Service, then was a quiet, but impressive little place. At one time it was the main line stop for meals. It even had two or three hotels, some dozen or more homes, a roundhouse and a wye. Now the buildings were closed, and for the station and the Black Canyon Eating House, their work was done. The roundhouse had burned down long ago.

The water tank sat inside the wye, the main line and one leg crossing the Cimarron River on short trestles, with the tail of the wye an old-fashioned three-track yard under a grove of giant cottonwoods. Waiting for us there was the other little Mudhen, that coupled on the head end, and Mudhen #456 coupled on behind the caboose.

In the Gunnison Canyon on the Sapinero Branch out of Gunnison, the drifts would pile up, and on March 11, 1952 the D&RGW's last C-16 #268 was opening the branch. Ahead of the engine it pushed wedge snowplow car #09271, a one-of-a-kind item on the narrow gauge. Trailing the engine was a flanger car and two cabooses for sectionmen and the train crew. The train would plow to a halt, then back up, but in this instance the plow wouldn't back out, and the engine backed down the track a few hundred feet. It then uncoupled the cars, and after the sectionmen had scraped the rails with shovels to clear ice, the #268 then coupled to the wedge plow and backed it out. Another couple of tries with the plow and this particular drift was opened up; it then proceeded further on the 25-mile branch.

It was a bad day on March 11, 1952 for little C-16 #268 to open the snow-blocked Sapinero Branch. Still seven miles from Sapinero, and end of the branch, while passing through Cebolla siding, a new storm, a veritable blizzard, came out of the west, blowing more drifts onto the track behind the train. The #268 had to plow back to Gunnison in the storm.

Here, #268 pulls the last run on the Sapinero Branch on September 28, 1954. Because their cabooses had been given to Lake City, the crew used an outfit car. Out of sight at the right, the local schoolteacher had her classes out by the fence to see the last train depart. This site is now under 70 feet of water. This line was once the D&RGW's narrow gauge transcontinental trackage to Salt Lake City and Ogden, Utah. *Robert W. Richardson, collection of Mallory Hope Ferrell*

MAXIMUM ADJUSTED TONNAGE RATINGS

From	To	Class of Engine 148 No. of Engines 470-479	Class of Engine 125 No. of Engines 450-464	Class of Engine 112 No. of Engines 432	Class of Engine 93 No. of Engines 430, 431	Class of Engine 85 No. of Engines RGS 20, 22,25	Class of Engine 72-71-70 No. of Engines 417-429 554, 555 RGS 42	Class of Engine 70 No. of Engines 400-411 RGS 40, 41	Class of Engine 60 No. of Engines 200-286 RGS 3-17	Class of Engine 47 No. of Engines 166-177	Adjustment Factor
		Tons	Tons	Tons	Tons	Tons	Tons	Tons	Tons	Tons	
Poncha Junction	Marshall Pass	187	183	173	113		106	92	79	67	1
Buxton	Marshall Pass	187	183	173	113		106	92	79	67	1
Poncha Junction	Mayville						120	105	89	81	2
Maysville	Monarch						88	75	65	56	1
Mears Junction	Poncha Pass		183	173	113		106	92	79	67	1
Alamosa	Moffat-both ways		2030	2000	1560		1190	1190	1120	950	12
Moffat	Villa Grove		830	830	600		480	480	420	390	5
Villa Grove	Round Hill		520	520	380		300	300	270	230	3
Round Hill	Poncha Pass		280	250	175		160	140	120	110	2
Villa Grove	Orient						106	92	79	67	1
Orient	Villa Grove						460	460	440	360	5
Gunnison	Sargent	1000	950	875	625		555	505	450	410	5
Parlins	Pitkin						145	120	110	120	2
Gunnison	Crested Butte	660	630	570	410		360	340	290	270	4
Crested Butte	Floresta	300	290	275	190		170	150	130	120	2
Gunnison	Castleton						270	240	210	225	4
Castleton	Baldwin						180	155	140	150	3
Crystal Creek	Cerro Summit						106	92	79	67	1
Montrose	Cerro Summit						106	92	79	67	1
Crystal Creek	Gunnison						570	520	465	420	5
Sapinero	Lake City						295	260	225	250	4
Montrose	Ridgway						460	420	370	340	5
Ridgway	Ouray						230	205	180	165	3
Ridgway	Dallas Divide					115	106	92	79	67	1
Placerville	Dallas Divide					175	160	140	120	110	2
Placerville	Vance Junction					285	260	230	210	185	3
Vance Junction	Telluride					115	106	92	79	67	1
Vance Junction	Lizard Head					160	145	130	105	100	2
Rico	Lizard Head					175	160	140	120	110	2
Dolores	Rico					310	280	250	220	205	3
Dolores	Glencoe					325	295	265	235	210	3
Glencoe	Millwood					230	210	185	160	145	3
Mancos	Milwood					230	210	185	160	145	3
Mancos	Cima					230	210	185	160	145	3
Durango	Cima					230	210	185	160	145	3

Gunnison Division, October 7, 1923.

OPPOSITE: A stock extra west of Iola in September of 1952 has #278 pulling a dozn cars and a caboose.

In just a few minutes, watered and coupled up, we started up the 4% grade to Cerro Summit six miles ahead on a winding grade, where a C-21 by itself could only manage but three cars of coal and the caboose. We seemed to move along at a good 15 miles per hour; a couple of times the lead engines were broadside ahead after a sharp curve. The country was sagebrush-covered with hills and ranches, quite a change from the canyon.

Cerro Summit wasn't much, just a passing track and wye. Both Helpers ran ahead light, about five minutes apart. The descending view was impressive, with the Utah mountains in the distance, and in the foreground the dry, desert-like hills reached down toward Montrose 17 miles away by rail.

Nearing the foot of the 4%, as we approached the one-time Helper point at Cedar Creek with its wye, we crossed a "sliding hillside." Blamed on irrigation on the mesa to the south, enormous amounts of yellowish earth kept slowly sliding at this point. The railroad had given up trying to maintain a track there year-around, so at the end of spring stock season, they would remove the track, and then bulldoze a right-of-way in September and relay the track for the fall stock season for train movements. On June 1, 1949 the line from Cedar Creek to Sapinero was abandoned, largely because of this problem.

Arrival at Montrose late in the afternoon found me leaving that nice caboose, saying good-bye to the crew, and heading for the hotel and a bath of hot water and soap. I didn't even try then to explore the dual gauge yard at Montrose and the variety of engines at the run-through two-stall enginehouse. That could wait till tomorrow!

Montrose's Dual Gauge Yard

Montrose was one of the three dual gauge yards where the Narrow Gauge Circle connected with the standard gauge. Much smaller in size and activity than Alamosa and Salida, in its final years only about one freight a month was operated to and from Gunnison, the former main line of the original D&RG during the years 1882-1890.

South from the yard extended the 35-mile Ouray Branch, which also in the final years had infrequent operations as far as Ouray, but at Ridgway the connection with the Rio Grande Southern required fairly frequent need of trains from Montrose.

Although always a point where motive power accumulated and was serviced, the facilities were meager. A two-track run-through type enginehouse could handle two standard gauge and four narrow gauge engines, but in actual practice they were generally kept outside.

Coaling was done by hand from gondolas spotted outside the enginehouse. Water was from a city hydrant. A shed annex

THIRD DIVISION
SECOND DISTRICT
Gunnison and Grand Junction

	WESTWARD								EASTWARD				
THIRD CLASS	SECOND CLASS	SECOND CLASS	SECOND CLASS	FIRST CLASS	Distance from Denver	Time Table No. 100 (March 28, 1920) — STATIONS	Distance from Grand Junction	Siding Capacity in Cars / Passing Tracks	FIRST CLASS	SECOND CLASS	SECOND CLASS	SECOND CLASS	THIRD CLASS
363 Freight	321 Freight	361 Freight	357 Lake City Mixed	315 Marshall Pass Route Express					316 Marshall Pass Route Express	358 Lake City Mixed	362 Freight	322 Freight	364 Freight
Leave Daily Exc. Sunday	Leave Daily Exc. Sunday	Leave Daily	Leave Daily Exc. Sunday	Leave Daily					Arrive Daily	Arrive Daily Exc. Sunday	Arrive Daily	Arrive Daily Exc. Sunday	Arrive Daily Exc. Sunday
	7.00 AM			10.30 AM	288.64	**GUNNISON** RNWCYT (DiGu) — 0.0	135.55	Yard	5.00 PM			4.15 PM	
					288.64	C.&S. CROSSING — 5.83	135.55						
	7.20			f 10.41	294.47	HIERRO — 4.69	129.72	49	f 4.35			3.35	
	7.40			f 10.52	299.16	IOLA — 0.92	125.03	12	f 4.20			3.10	
	7.43			f 10.54	300.08	KEZAR — 7.09	124.11	30	f 4.17			3.00	
	8.10			f 11.12	307.17	CEBOLLA — 6.80	117.02	46	f 3.55			2.30	
	8.35		3.35PM 316	s 11.30 358	313.97	**SAPINERO** RDY (Sa) — 0.81	110.22	61	s 3.35 357	11.30AM 315		1.55	
	8.40		3.45PM	11.32	314.78	LAKE JUNCTION — 6.07	109.41		3.27	11.15AM		1.45	
	9.05			f 11.49	320.85	CURECANTI — 6.67	103.34	31	f 3.05			1.10	
	9.35			12.07 PM	327.52	CRYSTAL — 1.37	96.67	15	2.40			12.30	
	10.15			¶ 12.10 / 12.30 322	329.01	**CIMARRON** RDWCY (Rn) — 5.58	95.18	52	¶ 2.35 / 2.15			12.10PM 315	
	11.05 322			s 1.00	334.59	CERRO SUMMIT — 6.68	89.60	20	1.57			11.05 321	
	11.45			s 1.25 316	341.27	CEDAR CREEK — 5.09	82.92	46	s 1.25 315			10.00	
	12.10 PM			f 1.40	346.36	FAIRVIEW — 5.15	77.83	47	f 1.07			9.30	
	12.35			1.55	350.50	OURAY JUNCTION — 1.01	73.69		12.53			9.10	
1.00PM	12.45 PM 316			2.05 / 2.20	351.51	**MONTROSE** RDWCY (Ms) — 5.88	72.68	Yard	12.50 321 / 12.30			9.00 AM	9.30AM
1.30				f 2.34	357.39	MENOKEN — 4.82	66.80	28	f 12.12				8.55
2.00				s 2.46	362.21	OLATHE (Ho) D — 5.28	61.98	28	s 12.01 PM				8.30
2.30				f 2.58	367.49	CHIPETA — 5.32	56.70	29	f 11.47				8.00
3.00PM		12.30 PM		s 3.20	372.81	**DELTA** RDWCY (Dt) — 4.72	51.38	Yard	s 11.35		10.10 AM		7.30PM
		12.55		f 3.31	377.53	ROUBIDEAU — 2.66	46.66	30	f 11.20		9.31		
		1.10		f 3.37	380.19	STRATTER — 4.65	44.00	41	f 11.15		9.20		
		1.30		f 3.48	384.84	ESCALANTE — 6.08	39.35	32	f 11.05		8.55		
		2.00		f 4.03	390.92	DOMINGUEZ W — 6.75	33.27	50	f 10.51		8.30		
		2.40		f 4.20	397.67	BRIDGEPORT — 5.16	26.52	41	f 10.35		8.00		
		3.10		f 4.31	402.83	DEER RUN — 5.13	21.36	35	f 10.23		7.30		
		3.35		f 4.43	407.96	KAHNAH — 3.84	16.23	16	f 10.11		7.05		
		3.55		s 4.52	411.80	WHITEWATER W — 5.46	12.39	71	s 10.02		6.50		
		4.25		f 5.02	417.26	UNAWEEP — 6.93	6.93	31	f 9.50		6.30		
		5.00 PM		5.20 PM	424.19	**GRAND JUNC.** RNWCYT (Jn)	(135.55)	Yard	9.35 AM		6.00 AM		
Arrive Daily Exc. Sunday	Arrive Daily Exc. Sunday	Arrive Daily	Arrive Daily Exc. Sunday	Arrive Daily		(135.55)			Leave Daily	Leave Daily Exc. Sunday	Leave Daily	Leave Daily Exc. Sunday	Leave Daily Exc. Sunday
(2.00) 10.65	(5.45) 10.93	(4.30) 11.40	(.10) 4.86	(6.50) 19.85		...Time Over District... / ...Average Miles Per Hour...			(7.25) 18.29	(.15) 3.24	(4.10) 12.33	(7.15) 8.67	(2.00) 10.65

SPECIAL INSTRUCTIONS

B-1. EASTWARD TRAINS ARE SUPERIOR TO WESTWARD TRAINS OF THE SAME CLASS.

B-2. No train will leave Gunnison, Cimarron, Montrose, Delta or Grand Junction without clearance.

B-3. Water tank at Elk Creek 5 miles west of Kezar.

B-4. Passenger trains will not exceed a speed of 15 miles per hour and freight trains 10 miles per hour down grade between Cerro Summit and Cimarron and Cerro Summit and Cedar Creek.

B-5. Westward freight trains will stop at Cedar Creek 10 minutes to cool wheels and inspect train.

B-6. Water crane at MP 320.44.

B-7. Lake City Branch trains when more than 15 minutes late will protect against main line trains between Sapinero and Lake Junction.

B-8. All trains must stop at Cerro Summit for inspection of train and brakes.

B-9. Passenger trains will not exceed 15 miles per hour, and freight trains 10 miles per hour through Bridgeport tunnel, near MP 400, and between slow boards between MP 403 and 404.

B-10. Telegraphones located Cebolla, Sapinero, Curecanti, Cimarron, Cerro Summit, Cedar Creek, Montrose, Delta, Dominguez, Bridgeport and Whitewater.

PREVIOUS PAGE. In the depths of the Black Canyon, with the walls of rock towering as much as 2,000 feet above the track, Engine #361 works the last excursion eastbound on May 30, 1949. The line west of Sapinero was abandoned that summer including Cimarron and Cerro Summit trackage. This had been the main line of the D&RG from 1882 when it was opened until 1890 when a new standard gauge line was opened from Glenwood Springs to Grand Junction. For many years passenger trains carried an open observation car from Gunnison to Cimarron.

ABOVE. With abandonment of the line through the Black Canyon, the D&RGW contracted to have the line torn up from Cedar Creek to Sapinero, 25 miles, including about 12 miles deep in the canyon along the river. Rails and other scrap were hauled to Sapinero using "little Mudhen" #360, a Class C-21 outside-frame 2-8-0. In this scene workmen prepare to take up Cimarron yard on July 7, 1949.

RIGHT. One last excursion was operated through the Black Canyon on May 30, 1949, the line being abandoned as of June 1. Here it is near the siding at Curecanti. Much of the canyon route had walls a thousand or more feet above the track. For a few years after abandonment, the grade was maintained as an access road for fishermen, but eventually dams were built and the grade flooded. Engine #361, a 1900 2-8-0, with nine cars, mostly cars to be used that summer on the Silverton Branch, is seen here. The *Silver Vista* is on the rear.

The last passenger train through the Black Canyon of the Gunnison is at Chepeta Falls on May 30, 1949. The occasion was a Rocky Mountain Railroad Club special from Gunnison to Cimarron and return. *Robert W. Richardson, collection of Mallory Hope Ferrell*

OPPOSITE TOP. The #361 leads an excursion in the Black Canyon of the Gunnison on a Rocky Mountain Railroad rail tour in September of 1948. *Robert W. Richardson, collection of Mallory Hope Ferrell*

OPPOSITE BOTTOM. The Rocky Mountain Railroad Club special with #361 nears the Curecanti Needle in 1949. The Curecanti Needle appears on the cover of the July, 1887 D&RGW public timetable. *Robert W. Richardson, collection of Mallory Hope Ferrell*

RIGHT. After the track through the Black Canyon was torn up in 1949, the grade was turned into a "fisherman's road" using the bridges left behind. A few years later, dams were built in the canyon, one just west of the site of Lake Juntion and the other very close to where the railroad left the Black Canyon via Cimarron Canyon. The water backed up almost to Gunnison, obliterating the grade.

FAR RIGHT. Gunnison Canyon was located between Gunnison and Sapinero, and for the entire distance the railroad, as in this scene, ran next to the river.

next to the enginehouse contained a few shop machines. Major work on locomotives was done at Gunnison and Ridgway, at the latter point until final receivership of the Rio Grande Southern.

A fairly modern depot at Montrose is now the county museum. Just north of it the wooden freighthouse was paralleled by a number of tracks for transfer purposes. The only modern equipment was a paving breaker used to ease the transfer of frozen concentrates. Otherwise the transfer work to the end was much as it was always, pick and shovel and wheelbarrows, with a plank being used between the two gauges of cars. Coal was hand shoveled!

The stock yards could handle quite a number of cars and was equipped to service the regular stock cars as well as the double deck sheep cars. Commencing in 1945 most livestock was transferred here, as the line to Salida was frequently cut by the Cedar Creek slide problem 10 miles east of Montrose.

Most livestock trains during the spring and fall rush came off the RGS loadings being made at Rico, Lizard Head and Placerville. The RGS would turn over the trains to the D&RGW at Ridgway, and a D&RGW crew with usually one Mudhen and caboose would be sent out for that purpose.

In June of 1949 the D&RGW abandoned the line from Sapinero through the Black Canyon to Cedar Creek, and after the abandonment of the RGS at the end of 1951, the Montrose operation was isolated from the balance of the narrow gauge lines. Retained were two Mudhens, #454 and #456, one Class C-18 #318, and C-19 #340. Only the #318 and #340 could be used on the lighter rails beyond Ridgway to Ouray. For a while there were loadings of iron ore and other commodities at Ridgway to keep one of the Mudhens busy.

The 10-mile track from Ouray Junction, a half mile south of the station, served very infrequently the needs of agricultural shipments from sidings, but all that remained at Cedar Creek was the wye. Since these shipments were to go on via standard gauge, it meant loading the cars for but a 10-mile or less trip, then having to be spotted at the transfer for loading into a standard gauge car. Railroad management discouraged loadings on this 10-mile section, once the Main Line East.

South of Montrose there was a large amount of sugar beets harvested, and these were hauled into Montrose in the approximately 60 coal cars which otherwise were occasionally loaded out two or three a month with ore at Ouray. The beets went to a plant at Delta and were transferred using a clamshell off-track crane.

With the distant Castle Peaks shrouded in clouds and snow, in the foreground 1882 Baldwin #278 2-8-0 with flanger car works slowly on one leg of the Castleton wye. On the other two legs of the wye the engine could pull the flanger, but on the "off" leg it had to back—and very carefully—as the wings of the flanger pulled snow onto the track, keeping the sectionmen busy. This February 28, 1950 trip was accomplished without a derailment. The track of the branch ended a few hundred feet beyond; it had been torn up a few years earlier to the third location of Baldwin, two and half miles up Ohio Creek. This entire track arrangement had been built by the Denver, South Park & Pacific in 1882, and beyond the tail of the wye some 17 miles of grading and rock work was completed in expectation of reaching Union Pacific coal lands beyond Ohio Pass. Only about a mile of track was ever laid.

Locomotive #278 readies for a trip from Gunnison to Baldwin by picking up a flanger car. It will take some dump gondolas to the Castleton loading point. The Baldwin coal was very good household fuel, and most of the cars were taken to points on the Valley Line and to Alamosa. Abandonment of the Valley Line in February of 1951 virtually ended operations on the Baldwin Branch.

One of the last two Class C-16 2-8-0 #278s takes on water at Castleton on the Baldwin Branch on February 28, 1950. This had originally been trackage of the Denver, South Park & Pacific, and the tank had been built by the successor Colorado & Southern Railway before the D&RG took over operation of this isolated line of the C&S in 1911.

Engine #268 pulls the dismantling train on the Baldwin Branch at Castleton, Colorado in 1955. Note the bell is missing, "appropriated" by a luncheon club. This line was once the Denver, South Park & Pacific. *Robert W. Richardson, collection of Mallory Hope Ferrell*

The Black Canyon on the original D&RG main line narrow gauge was as much as 2,000 feet deep, the railroad using about 14 miles of the canyon between Sapinero and Cimarron. The line was abandoned on June 1, 1949. The tiny distant train is an eastbound excursion. In the foreground at right is the almost indistinguishable steel water "column" which obtained water by dropping its inlet into the small stream entering the canyon.

The Lake City Branch took off the main line at the eastern entrance to the Black Canyon. Engine #278 and a combine comprised the daily mixed in 1920. The line was abandoned in 1933, but a mining man for a while attempted operation with a motor car built at the Rio Grande Southern, but gave up, and the car was used in part to build Goose #2. *Don Heimburger collection*

Because the tail of the Cimarron wye could only accommodate the engine and five passenger cars, the September 19, 1948 excursion from Gunnison had to be wyed in two sections. The track ahead of the engine is the beginning of the 5 1/2-mile climb of twisting 4% grade to Cerro Summit. When this was the busy main line of the D&RG and for many years afterward, Cimarron was a Helper point, with many three-engine trains, and sometimes even four- and five-engine turns. The #361 could haul three loads and the caboose on this grade.

RIGHT. This is C-16 #268 as it appeared at the Chicago Railroad Fair in 1949. It was lettered for a mythical Cripple Creek & Tincup Railroad and featured a color painting on the side of the tender. After the fair it was put back in use at Gunnison with minimal repainting and its regular pilot, headlight and stack were restored.

ABOVE. Locomotive #268 returned from the Chicago Railroad Fair in 1950, and eventually the tender was re-lettered, but the Grande Gold paint scheme remained to the end of its use in 1955. The countryside was very dry during the fall of 1953, and the master mechanic from Grand Junction fabricated this very effective cinder-catching sleeve which fitted over the stack, with the usual screen at the top. The engine's bell had been taken by a luncheon club, and a farm bell was substituted. It's now on display with a short train in a pavilion in Gunnison.

RIGHT. Because of its light weight, Engine #268 was used extensively for branch line service. It was the last of the C-16 Class in D&RGW service. It hauled the last revenue train west of Gunnison. *Henry Bender, C.T. Felstead collection*

Every year the stockmen of the Powderhorn region southwest of Gunnison gathered their livestock shipment from Iola, about 11 miles west of Gunnison. A single train powered by heavier class locomotives handled the loads east of Gunnison, but only the little #268 dared venture on the light track to Iola. As shown here on October 9, 1952 working its best, the #268 doubled over 30 loads into Gunnison, the caboose behind the engine for crewman to be handy to at times sit on the pilot sanding the rails. This was the last time the Powderhorn would ship out by rail, the line being near abandonment. For these final trips and with the danger of setting fires in the dry countryside, at the last moment the divisional master mechanic literally devised a unique cinder catcher. It was in the form of a sleeve that fit over the stack but left space between the stack and inside of the sleeve. It worked well. See page 15 for a typical stock schedule.

A standard gauge freight would come in from Grand Junction twice a week, powered by one of the few Mikados the D&RGW rostered. The Montrose yard crew used this engine for switching, using an idler car when moving narrow gauge cars. This was unique to the Montrose Yard, as at Alamosa and Salida the standard gauge locomotives had three-position couplers or even a two-position air-actuated coupler.

Unique also at Montrose was the use of one of the narrow gauge engines with an idler car doing the switching. This brought on a most unusual switching arrangement when the standard gauge passenger train, *The Mountaineer*, terminated at Montrose.

The yard crew with idler would pull the train, engine and cars from the station to the Ouray Junction wye and spot the train on the off-leg where the changeover of position of third rail occurred. The Mudhen would then run around the other two legs of the wye and couple onto the Pullman observation to complete the operation and then pull the turned train back to the station. A union rule agreement forbade using just the train's engine to do this turning.

In the final years one of the two last early standard gauge 2-8-0 locomotives was kept at Montrose. Locomotive #605, new in 1889, was sold in the summer of 1951 to a coal company. The yard crew, however, favored the narrow gauge engines, and so #605 had been idle for years.

Elusive Freights

Though photos have eluded researchers, for many years even after it was no longer the main line, freights east from Montrose frequently employed three and four engines and sometimes even five. From Cedar Creek there were seven miles of 4% to the summit of Cerro Summit, 1,200 feet above Cedar Creek. Cedar Creek itself was about 900 feet higher than Montrose.

In 1917 the D&RG bought five 2-8-0s from the stored equipment of the vanished Florence & Cripple Creek Railroad (and a sixth in 1920). This new fleet of six was assigned to Montrose and spent years working the line to Gunnison. Freights on this portion of the line included occasional Mudhens as far as Cimarron and the two ex-Crystal River engines, which became Class C-21s.

At first the ex-F&CC engines were classified as Class 70s along with the 1881 engines of that class, but eventually the F&CC engines were termed Class 72 until the renumberings of 1923.

In November of 1948 a strange change of engines occurred at Montrose. Down to just #317 and #318, the #317 needed a lot of boiler work. The #318 had worn out its running gear and was in need of shopping. With the aid of the hostlers and the sectionmen, the two were combined into one engine, which kept the number 318, then the boiler of #317 and the running gear of #318 were loaded out for scrap.

Montrose ended its narrow gauge functions in March of 1953, when the line from Ridgway to Ouray was abandoned, and the remainder of the branch was standard gauged.

Wedge plow #09271 was a reinforced wooden gondola loaded with rock and equipped with a large plow pilot such as had been used on locomotives. It was employed for years in the Black Canyon where a rotary, account of rocks, dared not be used. Here it is stuck on March 11, 1952 in Gunnison Canyon. Engine #268 will drop its train and then will come up and buck snow with the plow until the drifts are opened.

An eight-car train clanks and bobbles down the Ouray Branch with #318 traveling southbound near Dallas on April 17, 1952. *Robert W. Richardson, collection of Mallory Hope Ferrell*

The same train, but with seven cars, leaves Ouray. The small Ouray turntable is at right. *Robert W. Richardson, collection of Mallory Hope Ferrell*

Ouray enjoys a unique location in Colorado, sitting in a bowl surrounded by steep mountains. The D&RG narrow gauge reached the town in 1887 via a branch south from Montrose.
Clayton Tanner

OURAY, COLORADO

W 1571

This is Ouray, showing the Million Dollar Highway at upper center as it starts its climb to Red Mountain Pass. Railroad passengers traveled by stage from Ouray to the northern end of Otto Mear's Silverton Railway at Ironton. The gap was surveyed for a railroad, but besides requiring excessive grades, the economic crash of 1893 ended such ideas.

This short, three-car train with #454 pulling speeds southbound between Montrose and Eldredge on the Ouray Branch on November 21, 1951. *Robert W. Richardson, collection of Mallory Hope Ferrell*

The Ouray Branch

To observe and photograph activity on the Ouray Branch while I lived at Alamosa meant that it would be a very long day, beginning before daylight and often not ending until I got home way after midnight (with a roadside nap somewhere for an hour or two).

The 35-mile branch could provide all kinds of weather on the same day. It might be clear and sunny at Montrose, raining at Ridgway and snowing heavily at Ouray. It followed the Uncompahgre River; the first 25 miles to Ridgway was mostly open ranch country. The 10 miles to Ouray had steep grades as the valley narrowed and entered the mountains.

Most switches in the small yard still were of the stub type with harp stands. A turntable with worn out bearings required crew and bystanders' best efforts in turning the engine. There was no water tank, just a standpipe.

The engine crew preferred #318 as they claimed #340 was a rough-riding engine, showing the difference between engine classes that had long and short main rods. Engine #318's tender rode so rough the crew used that of the #340 for the final years. The master mechanic at Grand Junction simply told the machinist at Montrose, Bob Lutkiewicz, to get along the best he could with maintenance; in short he was "on his own." At some time in those final years someone had let the water get too low,

Locomotive #318 was the last Class C-18 2-8-0 with a stock train on the Ouray Branch. Each spring and fall the branch handled many such trains to and from the Rio Grande Southern.

This is the "draw," or changeover as it was termed, in the wye at Ouray Junction just outside Montrose. Trains of either gauge could pass through, but when cars of both gauges were coupled, the engine would have to be taken around the wye and recoupled. New officials at Denver couldn't understand this necessity when the relative position of the third rail had to change position. One official insisted and ordered a narrow gauge train crew to go around the wye without uncoupling from their standard gauge passenger train and a bad derailment was only averted at the last minute.

and the crownsheet showed signs of "pulling" the stays. With no hostler or watchman on duty overnight, an unexpected small leak in piping no doubt was the cause of some near fatal damage to the locomotive.

Mining traffic from Ouray had dropped to perhaps a couple of cars of rock ore of low value, once or twice a month. By the 1950s virtually all mining activity had ceased in that once very busy area.

AROUND THE CIRCLE. Tickets are on sale from Denver, Colorado Springs and Pueblo at $28.00. "Around the Circle" via Alamosa, Durango, Ridgway and Gunnison, and $33.00 via Alamosa, Durango, Ridgway and Grand Junction, going either direction. In connection with this trip various side trips can be made at reduced fares. This is a tour of 1,000 miles through the Rocky Mountains and is unsurpassed anywhere in the world.

Holders of Utah or Pacific Coast Tickets (the limits of which will permit) desiring to go via Alamosa, Durango and Rico, may have their coupons between Denver and Grand Junction exchanged upon payment of $10.00 to Ticket agent at Denver, Colorado Springs, Pueblo or Salida on the Westbound Trip; on the Eastbound Trip upon payment of like amount to the Agent at Grand Junction or Montrose.

D & R G W Form 3250
Sec. 8 Page 81
D & S L Form 1196

Alamosa Sept 23 1944

TRAIN ORDER No. *49* *Eng 456*

To *X E Eng 456*

At *Montrose* X Opr. M.

Eng 456 run extra Montrose to Ridgway

LSL
Chief Dispatcher

CONDUCTOR, ENGINEMAN AND REAR TRAINMAN MUST EACH HAVE A COPY OF THIS ORDER

Made *Com* Time *623 P* M. *Cowan* Opr.

D & R G W Form 3250
Sec. 8 Page 81
D & S L Form 1196

Alamosa Sept 22 1944

TRAIN ORDER No. *9* *Eng 463*

To *X E Eng 463*

At *Montrose* X Opr. M.

Eng 463 run extra Montrose to Cimarron

LSL
Chief Dispatcher

CONDUCTOR, ENGINEMAN AND REAR TRAINMAN MUST EACH HAVE A COPY OF THIS ORDER

Made *Com* Time *515a* M. *Cowan* Opr.

OURAY BRANCH.

315 Daily	Miles	STATIONS 5-19-1912	316 Daily
12 01	0.0	.... Montrose	12 01
....	0.6	.... Ouray Junction	....
f 3 20	8.0	.... Uncompahgre	f 11 26
f 3 32	12.3	.... Colona	f 11 15
f 3 40	15.1	.... Eldredge	f 11 07
....	22.5	.... Dallas	....
4 20	25.5	ar .... Ridgway lv	10 40
4 20	25.5	lv .... Ridgway .... ar	10 40
f 4 33	28.6	.... Piedmont	f 10 15
10	35.9	.... Ouray	9 50

OPPOSITE TOP. Crews doing switching at Montrose employed either standard or narrow gauge engines to do the yard work. Mikado #1202 used an idler car to enable coupling to narrow gauge cars.

THIRD DIVISION
OURAY BRANCH
Montrose and Ouray

WESTWARD						EASTWARD	
SECOND CLASS	FIRST CLASS	Distance from Denver	Time Table No. 100 March 28, 1920	Distance from Ouray	Siding Capacity in Cars Passing Tracks	FIRST CLASS	SECOND CLASS
341 Freight	319 Ouray Passenger		STATIONS			320 Denver Passenger	342 Freight
Leave Daily Exc. Sunday	Leave Daily					Arrive Daily	Arrive Daily Except Sunday
8.15 **PM**	2.25 **PM**	351.51 Ms	MONTROSE RDWCY	35.90	Yard	12.20 **PM**	4.10 **PM**
8.30	2.27	352.16	OURAY JUNC.	35.25		12.10 **PM**	4.00
9.00	f 2.48	359.54	UNCOMPAHGRE	27.87	18	f 11.45	3.19
9.20	f **2.59** 342	363.84	COLONA	23.57	21	f 11.33	**2.59** 319
9.30	f 3.05	366.50	ELDREDGE	20.91	17	f 11.24	2.40
10.10	f 3.25	374.36	DALLAS Y	13.05	27	f 11.00	2.10
10.50 320	s 3.45	377.08 Wy	RIDGWAY DWCY	10.33	Yard	s **10.50** 341	2.00
11.10	f 3.58	380.09	PIEDMONT W	7.32	17	f 10.27	1.35
12.10 **PM**	4.40 **PM**	387.41 Ay	OURAY RDWCT		Yard	10.05 **AM**	1.00 **PM**
Arrive Daily Exc. Sunday	Arrive Daily		(35.90)			Leave Daily	Leave Daily Exc. Sunday
(3.55)	(2.15)		........Time Over District.......			(2.15)	(3.10)
9.17	15.96		....Average Miles Per Hour....			15.96	11.34

Distances between stations: MONTROSE–OURAY JUNC. 0.65; OURAY JUNC.–UNCOMPAHGRE 7.38; UNCOMPAHGRE–COLONA 4.30; COLONA–ELDREDGE 2.66; ELDREDGE–DALLAS 7.86; DALLAS–RIDGWAY 2.72; RIDGWAY–PIEDMONT 3.01; PIEDMONT–OURAY 7.32

SPECIAL INSTRUCTIONS

H-1. EASTWARD TRAINS ARE SUPERIOR TO WESTWARD TRAINS OF THE SAME CLASS.

H-2. No train will leave Montrose or Ouray without clearance.

H-3. Water Tank at Cow Creek, between Eldredge and Dallas.

Because of rocks mixed with snow in the Black Canyon, this plow car was used. It was loaded with rock to weigh it down.

Standard gauge #1202 switches the Montrose yard. In this photograph, #1202 transfers two narrow gauge reefers that were loaded only five or six miles out of town on the remnant of the narrow gauge main line.

THIRD DIVISION
LAKE CITY BRANCH
Lake Jct. and Lake City

Westward SECOND CLASS 357 Mixed	Distance from Denver	Time Table No. 100 March 28, 1920 STATIONS	Distance from Lake City	Siding Capacity in Cars Passing Tracks	Eastward SECOND CLASS 358 Mixed
Leave Daily Exc. Sunday					Arrive Daily Exc. Sunday
3.45 PM	313.97	Sa SAPINERO DCY	36.56	79	11.15 AM
		0.81			
f 4.50	314.78	LAKE JUNC.	35.75		f 10.05
		13.22			
f 5.00	328.00	MADERA W	22.53	6	f 9.55
		1.82			
f 5.45	329.82	GATE VIEW	20.71	41	f 9.10
		9.72			
6.40 PM	339.54	YOUMAN	10.99	31	8.20 AM
		10.99			
	350.53	LAKE CITY WCY		31	
Arrive Daily Exc. Sunday		(35.75)			Leave Daily Exc. Sunday
(2.55)		........Time Over District.......			(2.55)
12.26		....Average Miles Per Hour....			12.26

SPECIAL INSTRUCTIONS
J-1. EASTWARD TRAINS ARE SUPERIOR TO WESTWARD TRAINS OF THE SAME CLASS.

J-2. Telegraphone Lake City.

This is the plain vanilla enginehouse at Montrose in April of 1952 with #318 simmering near the open door. The two-track structure featured dual trackage. *Robert W. Richardson, collection of Mallory Hope Ferrell*

This view shows both gauges of trains at Montrose on November 21, 1951. Narrow gauge switch engine #454 will use the idler car to turn the *Mountaineer* on the wye. Under some unusual union agreement the switch crew could not just run the standard gauge train around the wye. It was a constant source of argument until the *Mountaineer* was discontinued a few months later.

A short freight leaves Montrose on November 21, 1951 for Ridgway. The first two cars are loaded with roundhouse cinders for ballast purposes, and the two box cars will be handled by the Rio Grande Southern to Durango. The train will bring the last revenue loads off the RGS into Montrose, cars of concentrates from Rico and Ophir.

This is the end of the track, the uppermost switch in the Ouray yard. The stub switches and their ancient "harp" switchstands were relics of long ago. Though the day for this last run had been sunny at Montrose 35 miles to the north, a heavy snowstorm greeted its arrival at Ouray. From this point Otto Mears had surveyed a line in 1889 to later connect with his Silverton Railroad a few miles to the south, but the grades would have been impractical even though new electric trolleys were considered. Engine #318, which survived abandonment of the Florence & Cripple Creek Railroad, earlier hauled the last train on the Pagosa Springs Branch. The locomotive is now being rebuilt at the Colorado Railroad Museum.

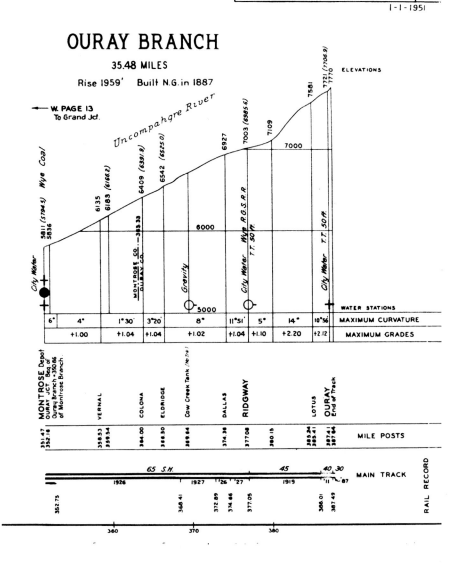

OURAY BRANCH

35.48 MILES

Rise 1959'   Built N.G. in 1887

W. PAGE 13
To Grand Jct.

Uncompahgre River

ELEVATIONS

WATER STATIONS

	6°	4°	1°30'	3°20'	8°	11°51'	5°	14°	10°56'	MAXIMUM CURVATURE
		+1.00	+1.04	+1.04	+1.02	+1.04	+1.10	+2.20	+2.12	MAXIMUM GRADES

MILE POSTS

MAIN TRACK

RAIL RECORD

Engine #318 does the final switching at Ouray, clearing the small yard of several ore cars that had been left for the last mining customer. The last train also removed the "depot" to Montrose, consisting of two box cars which had served in that capacity ever since the handsome building had burned.

On a wintery March 21, 1953 Engine #318 is being turned for the last time on the Ouray turntable as it makes the final run on that branch. In the summer, turning the engine was something tourists enjoyed watching, and crews would enter into the spirit of the day by letting kids "help" them turn the engine.

Conductor John Collett hands up orders for a final run to Ouray on March 21, 1953. The engineer was C.L. "Clayt" Braswell, senior engineer with rights on the narrow gauge lines at Gunnison as well. Upon completion of the run, the trackage into Ouray was abandoned, and the remaining 25 miles from Ridgway to Montrose was immediately standard gauged. Locomotive #318's bell was unable to ring mournfully for the occasion, as the clapper had fallen out and the bell got stuck (it was thought someone tried to steal the bell). The other men shown are Trainmen Joe Mazza and John Chiodo, and Fireman F.B. Wright.

From their acquisition in 1916, the ex-Florence & Cripple Creek locomotives were mostly assigned to working out of Montrose on the old main line to Gunnison and the Ouray Branch. Three years after this photo was taken on October 10, 1945, the #317's boiler was in need of major repairs, but the running gear was in good condition, while the #318 was in just the opposite condition. In the two-track enginehouse in the background, the foreman and a small crew of hostlers and sectionmen combined the #318's boiler with the #317's frame and cylinders.

Auction Fizzle. After attempting to auction the engines, rolling stock and other items of the former Ouray Branch, #318 was loaded for shipment to Grand Junction to await disposition. Mudhen Mikado #454 at right was scrapped and the boiler sold to a factory. This photo was taken at Montrose in April of 1953.

Car B-8 was moved from Grand Junction in 1962.

Business car K (B-8) was used on the Gunnison Division between 1923-1925. Note the drumhead on the rear platform.

When the D&RGW superintendent traveled to Grand Junction, the trucks of Business car B-8 (originally "K") were changed to standard gauge at Montrose. The car was built in 1887 for use by a superintendent during construction to Glenwood and Aspen and was carried in those work trains. It was sold to the Uintah Ry. in 1927 for occasional use by officials of the Gilsonite Co. It's now on display at the Colorado Railroad Museum in Golden.

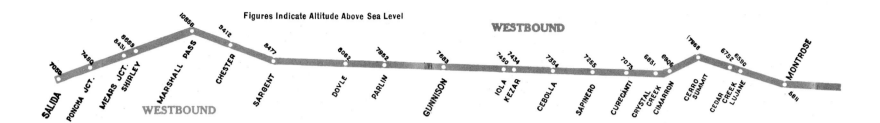

Figures Indicate Altitude Above Sea Level

WESTBOUND

WESTBOUND

SALIDA 7098
PONCHA JCT. 7490
MEARS JCT. 8431
SHIRLEY 8669
MARSHALL PASS 10856
CHESTER 9412
SARGENT 8477
DOYLE 8062
PARLIN 7952
GUNNISON 7683
IOLA 7450
KEZAR 7434
CEBOLLA 7354
SAPINERO 7255
CURECANTI 7075
CRYSTAL CREEK 6831
CIMARRON 6906
CERRO SUMMIT 7888
CEDAR CREEK 6752
LUJANE 6590
MONTROSE 5811

TRAIN via MARSHALL PASS and BLACK CANYON
(MAIN LINE NARROW GAUGE)

315	Mls. Fm Denver	Stations and Descriptive Notes
AM 5 10 6 30	216	**ar. SALIDA lv.** As previously explained, from Salida the Denver & Rio Grande continues overland westward by narrow gauge as choice. At Montrose the standard gauge is resumed, and at Grand Junction the routes come together again. Thence to Ogden, western terminal of the system, the track is standard gauge, as usual. Out of Salida by the narrow gauge route the train crosses the Arkansas by a splendid iron bridge.
s 6 45	220	**lv. PONCHA JUNCT.** On the right the Arkansas Valley forms a beautiful vista. Five miles from Salida the Poncha Hot Springs resort is passed; and having threaded pretty Poncha
s 7 10	227	**lv. MEARS JUNCT.** Pass, at Mears Junction the long ascent of the famous Marshall Pass is begun.
s 8 30 8 40	240	**ar. lv. MARSHALL PASS** Skirting Mt. Shavano, with Mt. Ouray (extinct volcano) opposite, climbing 211 feet with every mile onward led by a succession of sweeping billowy curves embracing magnificent reaches of heavy timber and grassy slopes, the train attains the crest, 10,856 feet aloft. This is the top of the Continental Divide—the watershed between the Atlantic and the
s 9 40	258	**lv. SARGENT** Pacific. From an observatory, erected here for the benefit of the travelers, an inspiring view of the jumbled Rockies is given. After a brief halt the train proceeds with
f 10 08	270	**lv. DOYLE** brakes partly set, on the serpentine descent before. The track presently encounters Tomichi Creek, and follows
s 10 24	277	**lv. PARLIN** it amidst a pleasant meadow country bordered by sagy hills, checkered with ranches, and fascinating for the trout-fisher and the hunter. The several little stations are sportsmen's outfitting places. Ten miles by stage from Doyle are the Waunita hot springs.
s 10 50 10 55	289	**ar. lv. GUNNISON** Population 1,500. This is the commercial center of the Gunnison Valley, and is the depot for important coal and mineral interests, which lie northward and are tapped by a branch line of the Denver & Rio Grande running 27 miles to Crested Butte in the picturesque Elk Mountains. Near
f 11 20	300	**lv. IOLA** Gunnison the Taylor and East rivers join and form the Gunnison; the town is a favorite angler's headquarters. The track,
f 11 40	308	**lv. CEBOLLA** westward heading, now follows the Gunnison down its valley, through a lush hay section, past many sportsmen's lodges devoted to anglers (for the Gunnison is one

Trains stop only at stations where time shown is preceded by "s" indicating "stop," or "f" indicating "flag."

315	Mls. Fm Denver	Stations and Descriptive Notes
AM		of the celebrated trout streams of the world), into a more broken country, to Sapinero and the Black Canyon.
s 11 56	314	**lv. SAPINERO** Here is the entrance to the Black Canyon of the Gunnison—rival of the Royal Gorge. From here, also, a branch line runs up Lake Fork Canyon, just beyond the station, on the left, 36 miles to Lake City, and Lake San Cristoval, the entrancing.
PM f 12 15	328	**lv. BLACK CANYON OF THE GUNNISON** At Sapinero an open-top observation car is attached during the season which permits, and immediately the train plunges into the Black Canyon of the Gunnison, to penetrate it almost 16 miles. This canyon, with prevailing color tones of brown and gray, is lashed by the deep, impetuous river. The train crosses and recrosses. The canyon walls reach a height of 2,000 feet, and are characterized by many rifts and by great masses of slide rock. Two well-known features are Chipeta Falls, which burst out high upon the wall to the right, and Curecanti Needle, an isolated needle
s 1 00	329	**lv. CIMARRON** spire, on the left. Finally, the railroad leaves the Black Canyon by the side Canyon of the Cimarron, emerging at Cimarron station, where dinner is waiting. Entering the mesa country of the western slope of Colorado, beyond Cimarron, the train, behind two engines, climbs the difficult grade of Squaw Hill. At
s 1 35	335	**lv. CERRO SUMMIT** the top, Cerro Summit, a wondrous view lies spread before; the Uncompahgre Range, the fertile Uncompahgre Valley, and Utah blue in the background. An undulating descent is made, amidst scrub oak and other sparse verdure; the vast valley works of the Gunnison Tunnel project put through by the United States Government Reclamation Service are passed, and the train is fairly in the midst of the rich fruit district of the Western Slope.
s 2 45	352	**lv. MONTROSE** Population 3,500. Here connection is made with Branch Line for the mining region of Ouray, Silverton, Telluride and Durango, south. The town is located in the Uncompahgre Valley; hay, grains, fruits and garden truck abound. The Gunnison Tunnel irrigation project, which will be completed in July, is bringing 150,000 acres more land under cultivation. From Montrose to Grand Junction the track is standard gauge; with snowy ranges to the east and south and the Grand Mesa outlined to the north, the train continues down the Uncompahgre River into the northwest. Orchards and tracts of sugar beets are on every hand, supplanting the sage brush.

A.M. time in light type. P.M. time in black type.

Locomotive #454 Mudhen Class K-27 strikes a handsome pose at Montrose. A couple of these engines were kept at Montrose to handle trains to and from the Rio Grande Southern. Until 1949 they were also employed as Helpers between Montrose and Cimarron.